# FROM THE SHADOW OF THE BLUES

FROM THE
SHADOW OF
THE BLUES

# FROM THE SHADOW OF THE BLUES

## MY STORY OF MUSIC, ADDICTION, AND REDEMPTION

JOHN LEE HOOKER JR.
WITH JULIA SIMON

ROWMAN & LITTLEFIELD
*Lanham • Boulder • New York • London*

Published by Rowman & Littlefield
An imprint of The Rowman & Littlefield Publishing Group, Inc.
4501 Forbes Boulevard, Suite 200, Lanham, Maryland 20706
www.rowman.com

86-90 Paul Street, London EC2A 4NE

British Library Cataloguing in Publication Information Available

**Library of Congress Cataloging-in-Publication Data**

Names: Hooker, John Lee, Jr., 1952- author. | Simon, Julia, 1961-
Title: From the shadow of the blues : my story of music, addiction, and
   redemption / John Lee Hooker Jr.., with Julia Simon.
Description: Lanham : Rowman & Littlefield Publishers, 2025. | Includes
   index.
Identifiers: LCCN 2024025806 (print) | LCCN 2024025807 (ebook) | ISBN
   9781538186237 (cloth) | ISBN 9781538186244 (epub)
Subjects: LCSH: Hooker, John Lee, Jr., 1952- | Blues musicians--United
   States--Biography. | Ex-drug addicts--United States--Biography. | LCGFT:
   Autobiographies.
Classification: LCC ML420.H6356 A3 2025  (print) | LCC ML420.H6356  (ebook)
   | DDC 782.421643092--dc23/eng/20240612
LC record available at https://lccn.loc.gov/2024025806
LC ebook record available at https://lccn.loc.gov/2024025807

*To Mom, Dad, and Big Mama, thank you for putting up with what no family or parent should ever have to go through. Because of your long-suffering love; visits to jails, prisons, and hospitals; and picking me up over and over again out of the dirt in which I should have remained, because of you—and only by the grace and mercy of God—I am who I am today.*

"John Lee was unique. No one sounded like him. No one has ever tried. He was rhythm all in one chord, no fancy stuff. No fooling! His voice could frighten a ghost, and what he said was not dinner conversation. "Crawlin' Kingsnake," "Boom Boom," and "Boogie Chillen": these aren't songs by someone looking for a chart topper. But they did top the charts! Unique because there is nothing like him. He doesn't fit into the neat little boxes musicians are often forced into. It feels as if you are being put in touch with music before recording, before technology demanded a format. He stands alone. If you got the chance to play with him, you realized there was no compromise. You played with him—he didn't play with you. I was privileged to be there. *I'm so happy to know that John Lee Hooker Jr. is following proudly in the preeminent footsteps of his amazing father!*"

**—Keith Richards, The Rolling Stones**

# CONTENTS

INTRODUCTION: SOLEDAD PRISON     1

PART 1: GROWING UP IN DETROIT     7

1    FAMILY AND EARLY FIGHTS     9

2    MONEY, CLOTHES, AND DRUGS     17

3    HEROIN, PROSTITUTES, AND
     FIRST ARREST AS AN ADULT     31

4    WAYNE COUNTY JAIL     43

PART 2: CULT DRUG PROGRAM AND
INCARCERATION     49

5    THE SYNANON CULT     51

6    JACKSON STATE PRISON AND
     CASSIDY LAKE     59

7    CALIFORNIA: CRIMES, HEISTS,
     AND THE CON GAME     67

PART 3: MUSIC, PRISONS, AND CON GAMES    77

8    CANADIAN TOUR AND PRISON     79

# CONTENTS

9   MARIE'S OVERDOSE AND SANTA
    RITA JAIL                                    85

10  CALIFORNIA REHABILITATION
    CENTER                                       91

11  ON THE RUN                                   97

12  BACK IN CRC, SOLITARY AT
    CHINO, AND GILROY                           105

13  BOXING AT CONSERVATION CAMPS   109

14  THE CON IN DETROIT: I'M SHOT    115

PART 4: REDEMPTION AND FALLS       121

15  BACK IN OAKLAND, I TURN TO
    THE LORD                                    123

16  MY FIRST FALL                              133

17  MY BAND IN REDWOOD CITY
    AND SECOND MARRIAGE                         141

18  MY FATHER'S DEATH AND MY
    THIRD AND FINAL FALL                        147

PART 5: FROM THE BLUES TO THE
GOOD NEWS                                       153

19  MUSICAL SUCCESS                            155

20  MY NEW LIFE IN MINISTRY                    169

21  SINGING ABOUT THE LORD                     181

22  SHARING LOVE AND LIFE IN
    GERMANY                                     187

NOTES                                           201

ACKNOWLEDGMENTS                                 205

ABOUT THE AUTHORS                               209

# INTRODUCTION

## SOLEDAD PRISON

After I was released from a Michigan prison stint in 1972, my dad invited me to live with him out in California so I could get back on my feet. When I arrived in Oakland, I was not surprised to see beautiful people of all races and nationalities coming by my dad's house almost daily; there is no need to wonder if I enjoyed my new home. One day, my dad shared some very exciting news: we were going to record a live show in the notorious Soledad Prison that housed Sirhan Sirhan, convicted of the assassination of Senator Robert F. Kennedy, and the Soledad Brothers, charged with the murder of a prison guard in January 1970.

These days, before anyone enters a correctional facility, the authorities run a thorough background check to see if the person has ever been arrested or convicted of a state or federal crime. Someone like me, with a prison record, would be barred from entry. Yet for some reason, I was allowed in to play the show. Ed Michel's production firm at ABC Records had set it up. When we arrived on June 11, 1972, it was very hot and dusty; all the inmates were grouped by ethnicity, nationality, race, and gang. My dad said to me, "Junior, this is your chance to go big time. I'm giving you this opportunity to establish your name. I want you to open up and do t-t-t-t-t-two songs."

I sang "Superlover" and "I'm Your Crosscut Saw." It was surreal. After I was introduced, the guys welcomed me with a loud round of applause and a "Go 'head, Junior Hooker. Sing, boy!" Before I left the stage, I introduced my dad, saying, "The Boogie Man." They rose to their feet as he hit a slow, signature John Lee Hooker–style blues song. It was literally standing room only; they loved that man called John Lee Hooker. I smiled as I watched. I was so proud of my dad. But at that moment, I also was sick as a dog from heroin withdrawal. I really just wanted to hurry up and get out of there so I could get paid and get some dope.

As I stood by the stage, watching my dad mesmerize the crowd, I dreamed, wondering if I could be just like him one day.

Fourteen years later, in 1986, I was sentenced to sixteen months at Soledad Prison for grand theft person. We drove up to the penitentiary through the thick fog, and I thought to myself, "Oh my God. There's the same gun tower." I saw the central yard, where we'd done the show, and emotion overcame me as I reflected back to June 11, 1972. It was the same sally port gate, but this time, I was driving in on the Gray Goose, the bus that transports prisoners throughout California, and I was chained around the waist, wrists, and ankles, like a recaptured runaway slave. After I went through all of the preliminary stuff to check in, I was summoned to see my counselor. He told me I would be going to a dorm in the south part of the prison to do my time; I was to report to my supervisor in the landscape department.

After I put my stuff up and fixed my bed, I headed for the supervisor's office, located inside a shed. The door was open, but I knocked before I went in. The supervisor looked up and said, "Come on in."

I asked, "Is this the landscape office?"

He said, "Yes, you've come to the right place."

The guard took my paperwork and asked for my prison ID; after seeing it, he looked up at me and said, "I'll be darned. I remember you."

I answered, "I've never been here before, sir. Maybe you've mistaken me for somebody else." When I said that, I was thinking from a prisoner's perspective: I hadn't done time there as an inmate.

"Oh yes, you have," he replied. He reached in his drawer and pulled out an eight-by-ten black-and-white photo with me onstage and him, Ernie, a skinny guard at the edge of the stage, from fourteen years earlier. The photo is the album cover of *Live at Soledad Prison*. I was blown away. If I had wanted to lie, I couldn't: he had the evidence in his hands.

Ernie gave me the best landscape job on the crew: he put me in the section where the officers live on the grounds. He said, "I'm going to put you in charge over there. You'll be cutting grass and making sure the guys are doing the right things. Conjugal visits are there. You'll be taking care of that. I'll keep you out of the old, dirty, and messy jobs around here."

Many years later, when the Lord had delivered me from dope and cleaned me up, I was back in the church and visiting prisons all over the United States, but there was one prison I longed to enter: the infamous Soledad. I prayed to be allowed back in to preach and testify to the power of God. Other chaplains, guards, and volunteers kept telling me, "You can't get into Soledad. If you've done time in there, it's going to be hard."

On the application, where it asked, "Have you ever done time here at Soledad?" I wrote, "Yes," and gave the years when I was an inmate there. I knew the God I serve could do anything; I prayed to be allowed in. When I saw the Lord open that door, I danced and shouted, "Hallelujah!" The scriptures say, "For the Lord God is a sun and shield; the Lord bestows favor and honor; no good thing does He withhold from those whose walk is blameless" (Psalms 84:11).[1]

I wanted people to see the glory of God. I was a dope fiend who'd had a gig to record at Soledad Prison, then it became my residence as a convict, and now I was going back as a chaplain of God to exemplify His amazing grace.

After I was cleared, I walked into Soledad South and saw the very dorm where I'd been housed and the yard where I'd taught Bible study. I was escorted to the central main yard, where we'd recorded, and then I entered the chapel to listen to the inmates preach and sing; I was smiling ear to ear. After the inmates finished speaking, I was invited up to the pulpit. I almost started to cry because I was experiencing something extraordinary—a miracle that only the Lord can perform. But I took a deep breath and testified about the year 1972, a date when some in attendance were not even born. I testified about when we'd recorded there and how, fourteen years later, I returned as a prisoner, and how I was now standing in the pulpit before them as a man of God, a chaplain who is saved, sanctified, and filled with the Holy Ghost. I told them God can do anything if you just follow Him faithfully. I expounded on the traps that were waiting for them upon their release and told them to be sure they were grounded in faith, to be serious about following God;

if not, I told them they would fail—either return to prison or die in the streets. I told them of my ups and many downs and of how I never gave up. They clapped and waved their hands in the air and glorified God. I left Soledad, and while driving in my car, I said, "Thank you, Jesus. Look where you have brought me from. Thank you, Lord, for opening the door that some said would never open up to me." It was one of the highlights of my ministry, being allowed to go back in there as a representative of the Kingdom of God. "For with God nothing shall be impossible" (Luke 1:37).

My name is John Lee Hooker Jr., the son of John Lee Hooker, the famous blues artist. My dad was born in the Mississippi delta into a family of sharecroppers. He left home as a teen to try to make it as a musician. First, he went to Memphis, then to Cincinnati and on to Detroit. He made his first hit record, "Boogie Chillen," in 1948. Even then, my dad had an original sound: he told stories about life and played the guitar with his own special groove. I was born in Detroit in 1952. When I came along, my dad and mom, Maude Ella Mathis (after she married my dad, Maude Ella Hooker), already had two daughters: Diane and Vera (later, Zakiya). After me came my younger brother, Robert, and my three younger sisters, Shyvonne, Karen, and Lavetta. Even though my dad was a successful musician, we didn't have much money growing up. Record companies took advantage of my dad, so we lived in low-rent houses. He could finally afford to rent a house around the time I first went to school, in the mid-1950s. Because my dad needed money for his family, he was on the road a lot, performing. He often stayed away for three or four weeks at a time, sending money back to my mom to pay the bills.

My dad became more famous when "Boom Boom" came out in 1962, which earned him some money and recognition. But back at home, I was growing up with a dad on the road and a mom who cheated while he was away. I turned to drugs to escape the pain and hurt in my family. Drugs led to crime—mostly thefts and burglaries to get money to feed my addiction. In 1969, when I was seventeen years old, I was arrested and sentenced to a drug program instead of prison time. My life for the next thirty years, give or take, was spent in and out of jails and prisons, doing time for crimes related to my dope addiction. Finally, I was released from prison for the last time in 1998; however, that was not the end of my drug habit: I had several falls before I was finally clean and sober. In 2003 I completed my final drug program. By then I had formed my own blues band and started touring throughout the United States. My first album, *Blues with a Vengeance*, was released in 2004, nominated for a Grammy Award, and won the W. C. Handy Award for Debut Artist. My third album, *All Odds Against Me*, released in 2008, also received a Grammy nomination.

For about ten years, I had a very successful career as a blues artist, touring all over the world: across the United States, Europe, Turkey, and even Russia. But after six albums, I decided to give up singing the blues and touring and devote myself fully to the Lord. I went back to school and became a chaplain to preach and minister to all, including those in the very prisons where I'd served time. Instead of singing blues, I turned my attention to gospel and the music that testifies to my experiences. I now preach, minister, and perform gospel music at events and in prisons in the United States and in Germany, where I am now living. My life story is one of ups and downs, successes and failures, but most especially of second, third, and fourth chances. I hope that it will provide faith, inspiration, and hope to those struggling with addiction and imprisonment, helping them to turn their lives around. My life testifies to the evil of drugs, but it also shows that everyone deserves the opportunity to try again. If the Lord can forgive me, then he can provide anyone who has faith a chance at redemption and salvation.

# 1

# GROWING UP
# IN DETROIT

# 1

# FAMILY AND
# EARLY FIGHTS

My earliest memories are from when I was four or five years old, growing up in Detroit in the early 1950s. It was lawless, violent, and corrupt. A police squad called the Big Four rode in unmarked black cars, striking fear in the hearts of every minority in the neighborhood. Police brutality and racial profiling were standard procedures. Police took bribes from drug dealers, loan sharks, fence men, and even pimps who didn't want their prostitutes arrested. Most Black people, poor Whites, and Asians—my family included—played the "numbers" (an illegal, Mafia-run gambling game).

We were a very close family: my father; mother; two older sisters, Diane and Vera (later, Zakiya); and my younger brother, Robert, lived on the west side, on Bangor Street. My grandmother, Big Mama (Addie Mathis), who lived on the east side and worked as a maid on the west side, would catch the bus to her job. She'd come over to babysit, hang out, cook, and play blackjack and bingo for pennies and nickels because, most of the time, my dad was on tour on the road and my mother worked downtown at Kresge Dime Store.

Like most children going to school for the first time, I was kind of nervous. Even though we lived around the corner from the school, my mother escorted me that first day. The teacher was kind and introduced me to the class. She told everyone to say hello to the new student, Johnny Hooker. Right off the bat, my eyes scanned the small room to see if I was in any danger. I felt the intensity of being in a class with different ethnicities and nationalities and especially with people who were bigger than me. I was accustomed to being around my siblings and people in the neighborhood and was nervous, thinking I had to stay there all day with people I didn't know. Everybody looked alright, and I had never been attacked, but still, it felt strange.

That first day, I came out of school with homework in my little book bag to show my family. I knew how to get home: walk out of the school, turn right, and there was my house. Back then was not like now, when parents pick up their kids because they're afraid they might be kidnapped. Suddenly, a big-headed boy I didn't know (named Ralph) came up and said, "Who do you think you are? What are you doing over here, boy?"

I answered, "Why, Wha-wha-wha-wha-what did I do?"

He had two or three guys with him, but I was paying attention to Ralph. He pushed me and said, "Did you hear me, boy?" I started running—all the way to the front door. Big Mama was in a rocking chair, watching cowboy movies; I could hear the bang, bang, bang. She walked up to the screen door, looked out at the boy who was chasing me, and said, "You better get your butt out there and fight him back, boy. And, no, you ain't getting in this house. If you don't get back down there and fight him, I'm gonna whup the mess out of you. Now, get down there."

My Big Mama was a big girl. She used switches from the bushes or trees, a belt, an extension cord, or even her shoes to punish me if I got sassy with her. *Bam!* She shut the screen door and made sure it was locked. I had to handle this big-headed boy, or she would handle me.

I put my book bag down, put on my mean face, and ran. I didn't even size him up. I grabbed him in a headlock and pulled him to the ground. I was imitating my hero Bobo Brazil, the Black wrestler on TV. The ground was muddy and wet because it had been raining. When I had him in a headlock, I saw a little hole full of mud, grabbed some, and shoved it in his mouth. I heard him cry out, "Stop it!"

Then Big Mama said, "Alright, let him go. Let him go, Junior."

She had been watching the whole time. She wasn't going to let anybody get hurt, but she wanted to make sure I defended myself. That standard has followed me all of my life, even to today.

The bully went home dirty, with mud all over his face. When my dad got home, he found out about it. Pretty soon he and this tall man were talking in front of our house. Ralph's dad said, "Your boy beat up my son for no reason at all, and he better not do it again, or he'll have to see me."

My dad looked up at him and said, "You tell yo boy, the next time he mess with my son, I'm going to come and see him and you too."

My dad had a speech impediment: "B-But you ain't g-g-g-g-g-gonna go do na-na-na-nothin to my boy. That's my son. Your boy came a r-r-r-r-round here and started it and chased my son home. And my son whupped him. Now, keep him away from here."

Before that I had only gotten into fights with my sisters and brother. This was my first real fight outside, my first violent act. This big-headed boy, who looked like he might've been in the first grade, had chased me home. I'd just started school, and this boy wanted to be a bully. Fighting him made me stronger; it taught me to defend myself. That's how it's always been in my family: you better fight, even if you get whupped. You don't run, you come on with it.

We lived in a gray house where the roof leaked because the wood was rotted and decayed; we had a bucket to catch the drops. From our backyard you could see down the alley: glassy, dirty, and smelly, with dead rats that a car might've run over. That was typical.

One day, I saw a gang of teenage boys beating up my older cousin Willie. I was four or five; what could I do to some eighteen- or nineteen-year-olds? All I could do was run and tell Big Mama what happened. I saw them beat up Willie from twenty yards away. He ran toward me until they quit chasing him, and then they threw bottles at him. I heard them breaking: *pow, pow!* He was crying. That was the first time I'd ever seen him cry, because he was an older dude, about eighteen. He had to go back to school the same way the next day, so Big Mama gave him a butcher knife. That was the last time I saw Willie until I'd grown up a little and moved to the east side.

I must admit I became a troublemaker—a class clown who always made the kids at Scripps Elementary School laugh with my silly antics. In 1963 I kept getting my classmate Edwin Titus in trouble. I would make faces and he'd burst into this loud, goofy laugh. The teacher would turn from the blackboard or lift her head up from checking homework, then make Edwin go stand in the corner. I always kept a straight face.

Mr. Palato, the principal, had salt-and-pepper hair and a fake smile. He always looked as though he only had one eye focused on you: "I'm watching you, Hooker." One time, when my teacher, Mrs. Adams, left her desk, I went inside the drawer and stole money. It wasn't much, but five dollars was big bank to me in those days. Sometimes, she would catch me talking during a test or cracking jokes during quiet time. As punishment, Mrs. Adams made me stand in the cloak room, where I'd then go inside the pockets and steal money. If I was lucky, I got a dollar bill and a gang of change. When being sent to the cloak room didn't deter me, I was sent to the principal's office.

Mr. Palato would yell, and people could hear him from far away: "Johnny Hooker, do you think getting an education is a joke, son?"

"No, sir."

"Oh yes, you do! Because your name keeps coming to my attention."

So that "it wouldn't happen again," he opened his desk and pulled out a miniature boat paddle with about six holes in it, then told me to bend over. With each contact with my butt, I would yell, "Ahhhh!" and he would say, "Am I making myself clear, Johnny?"

"Yes, sir." These days, he'd be arrested for child abuse or assault on a child. But back then, our parents knew this was going on and accepted it—at least most did—because the same thing had happened to them as children. My butt was stinging when I left that office. My classmates had heard the violence, and I could see the little smirks on all their faces as I entered the room.

Another boy in school, Calvin Robinson, and I were foes, and everyone knew it. We would get into confrontations in practically every class we attended together because we were jealous of each other. We constantly made challenges: "I can run faster," or "The waves in my hair are better." One day, during physical education, Mr. Redding, the gym teacher, was fed up with us and decided to settle it in class so that we wouldn't escalate. He asked, "Who has some boxing gloves they can bring to class next week?"

I had gotten boxing gloves as a Christmas gift, so I said, "I do."

"Okay, Johnny, bring them to school next week, and you can settle your squabbles. Okay?"

Calvin and I agreed. We were both confident we would be victorious.

Monday afternoon, the word was out: "You don't want to miss this: Johnny Hooker and Calvin Robinson are going to fight it out today with boxing gloves in the gym!"

Mr. Redding put a floor mat down so that if anyone got hit and fell to the floor, they wouldn't get hurt too badly. He gave us instructions: "After this, I don't want to ever see you two in each other's faces, or I will send you both home with a suspension from school. You understand?"

"Yes, sir," we both agreed.

There were no mouthpieces or grease put on our faces to protect us from cuts. It was all "Go for what you know." We squared off, Mr. Redding blew the whistle, and we began to fight. Calvin was a wild man. He swung for the fence without a plan for how to defeat me. I was a little more calculated, as I was a Cassius Clay fan. Move, jab, and then try to knock him out with my overhand right. The fight lasted only one round. I hit Calvin with a jab, a one-two punch, and shots to his body, and the teacher stopped it so he wouldn't get hurt. Calvin Robinson was crying because he'd lost the fight. Mr. Redding had us shake hands; there were never any problems between Calvin and me after that.

I was not all that bad, because Mr. Palato allowed me to join the school marching band. We had white helmets and marched during Parents' Day and for graduation. I was also chosen to be on the safety patrol. I had a helmet with a band across my shoulder and wrapped around my waist. Inspired by the safety patrol, I became a Boy Scout. They made me the treasurer. Dues were a dime a week, and I collected them. It was my job to turn the money in at the end of each month, but I didn't; I stole it all. I was the Judas who turned Jesus in for thirty pieces of silver. They fired me.

My dad would always say, "You make sure you get you a ba-ba-ba- ed-ed-education."

Both my parents always encouraged working hard, going to school, and going to church. They didn't go to church, but they would drop us off there. If my sisters Diane and Zakiya weren't babysitting and my mom wanted to go somewhere, they would drop us off at Sunday school. I don't think it had any effect on who I am today, or maybe it did, I don't know. At the time, I was never inspired by a message. As a matter of fact, I stole money out of the Sunday basket. I would pretend to put something in and then grab a dollar and pass the collection. Sometimes, when the preacher would be preaching up a storm, people walked up and threw money on the floor. My cousin Joe had a shoe where the sole was not stitched. I watched him go up to the pulpit and slide the money in his shoe, so I mimicked him. If Joe wasn't with me, I would tear my sole off and steal money.

My dad had a big hit with "Boom Boom" in 1962 on Vee-Jay Records. The song has a great riff and a strong groove that get you moving from the opening beat. The backing band was the Funk Brothers from Motown, with Joe Hunter on keys, James Jamerson on bass, Benny

Benjamin on drums, Hank Cosby on tenor sax, and Larry Veeder on guitar; they add so much life and energy to the track. Still, they keep my dad's performance front and center. My dad's lyrics tell a story of love and romance with attitude and confidence: "I'm gonna shoot you right down, right off your feet; take you home with me. . . . Boom, boom, boom, boom." No sign of his stutter here—just straight-ahead punch: "Boom Boom." The song made it to the Billboard R&B chart and even the Billboard Hot 100. My dad's signature sound was all over the country. Later, bands like the Animals and Big Head Todd and the Monsters covered "Boom Boom." It was even recognized on the Rock and Roll Hall of Fame's list entitled "The Songs That Shaped Rock and Roll."

Of course, my dad was the biggest thing in the neighborhood. He was huge. All the record stores had his song. Black Bottom, west side, east side, north side—"Boom Boom." He was the man. For some reason, people wouldn't call me Boom Boom, but they called me Bam Bam, and the nickname stuck.

I loved my papa so much; when he had to leave, I would say, "Daddy, please don't go."

He would answer, "I got to go, Junior. We got to pay the bills."

I would cry and cry when he left. My sisters and Big Mama would have to pull me away from him and hold me back. He would be gone three weeks, sometimes a month, and it killed me. I used to hug his suits in his closet and play his music and cry.

When he called from the road, I could hear this muffled sound. I could tell when he was overseas because I could hardly hear him, but I heard that distinctive voice. I would ask, "Daddy, when are you coming home?"

"I'll be home in two more weeks. And if y'all are good, I got something for you."

He was my buddy. One time, when he didn't want me to cry, he took me with him to Canada. I was maybe seven or eight years old. I was in the back dressing room, and I could see all the people. The women were screaming like he was Elvis Presley or Michael Jackson. He did this funny little dance when he got up with his guitar. He couldn't dance a lick, but whatever he did, they all loved him.

But taking me with him was not a good thing. He'd gotten me my own room, but I still walked into his room. Then a lady came in, and they started kissing passionately. I knew this wasn't right—this blonde was not my mother. I had never seen anything like this before. Because I was a kid, I started crying. I believe my dad told the girl, "I'll see you tomorrow, honey."

I blew his date. I'm sure he thought, "Junior ain't coming with me no more."

# 2

# MONEY, CLOTHES, AND DRUGS

When I was a little older, my family moved from Bangor Street to Jameson Street. My first experience there was with a neighborhood gang of boys—all Black except for one White boy, named Mickey Schneider. I was playing outside by myself when they came up and said, "Who are you, boy? What you doing out here? Where you come from?"

My answer was only silence. They mean mugged me and said, "Get him, Mickey." Mickey approached me, glaring, with a balled-up fist. I walked up, grabbed Mickey by the waist, picked him up, and threw him to the ground, then began to beat him up. That's when the oldest boy, Fred Bates, pulled me off him and said, "Ha-ha, what's your name, boy?"

I said, "Johnny Hooker."

Fred smiled and said, "You alright, Lil' Hooker. We had to check you out first."

I guess it was an initiation fight; after that, Mickey became one of my best friends. In fact, everybody in the neighborhood—Mickey, Fred, Gregory from across the street, and other guys who lived on different blocks—we all became a gang. My name was Lil' Hooker.

We lived next door to the Davis family, who had a girl named Rosemary and a young boy named Earl. Next door to them was the White family. Reverend White cautioned his daughters Brenda, Joann, and Linda to stay away from "them Hooker boys." He was a strict preacher. He advised them right: we were bad boys.

My dad would come back from out of town, and if we'd been good, he'd bring home travelers checks and give us forty or fifty dollars. We thought we were rich. Because Detroit was a fashion city, everybody

CHAPTER 2

dressed as sharp as a tack. Whoever dressed the best would attract the girls. My brother Robert and I would catch the bus downtown and put clothes on layaway, sometimes a long cashmere coat or a nice knit shirt. I would put five or ten dollars down on a pair of alligator shoes. At that time alligator shoes only cost one hundred dollars. My favorite shoe store was Ben B. Berke's; you could buy lizards, alligators, and crocodiles there. When I wore my alligators to school, all eyes were cast down at my feet: I knew I was sharp.

I hustled for money all around. I shoveled snow in the winter, cut grass in the summer, and raked leaves in the fall. I was also a paperboy. I even went with my best friend Ernest Smith, "Sugar Man," and we got jobs shining shoes on Kercheval Street. We were allowed to bring our own shoes and shine them for school or parties. We were both fond of dressing up. If you had a handmade gabardine shirt, matching colors, and shiny shoes, you were somebody. Thanks to a grease called Duke, a brush, and our mothers' or sisters' old stockings that we'd made into doo rags, we had waves for the babes. From the waves I graduated to a doo created with a kind of lye that burned your scalp if you didn't use enough Vaseline. It cost twelve dollars to get your hair done at Style-o-Rama or Wiggin' Willie's on Mack Avenue.

As a boy, I just loved to have a wad of money in my pocket. I even saved in a piggy bank. Those same practices are with me today. My sister Karen calls me Big Money because I hold on to it. I watched my dad make some smart real estate investments. He wasn't educated, but he knew how to buy a house and flip it for a profit. He would always say, "Save your money, boy. Ba-ba-ba-you better save it, because you ain't getting no more when that's gone."

I believe my work ethic came from my family. Big Mama worked as a maid in the rich folks' neighborhood; her boss was a lady named Mrs. Clydesdale. My mother worked downtown at Kresge Ten-Cent Store. In the beginning I hustled. When I got a little older, I got a little slicker. I wanted more money in my pocket and bigger paydays, but I was not old enough to work at a car factory. I paid about fifteen dollars to have a fake birth certificate made that "proved" I was eighteen years old. After that, I got jobs easily at Chrysler and Ford Motor Companies. I had a love of money at an early age—the love of buying clothes and taking the girls out to parties or to the movies, where I always got my first kiss when the lights went out.

When I was about ten or eleven, I went with my dad to Chicago, where he was performing at Robert's Show Lounge. First, he took me to meet his older brother and sister, who were living there; they were happy to meet me. Then he took me to the Robert's Hotel, where he got me my own room. He asked me, "Can you handle your own room, boy?" I told him, "Of course, I can. I'm a big boy." Then we went to his room; he said he had some friends coming over who wanted to meet me. We went in, and talk about the noise! People came in screaming. It was loud, like a family reunion or a free-for-all. I met Big Mama Thornton, Eddie Taylor, Jimmy Reed, everybody—the room was crowded, and I was just sitting over in the corner, watching all the fun. Big Mama reached around and pulled some liquor wrapped in a paper bag out of her pocket, cursing at everybody. Then she said, "Johnny, look at you. Is that your boy?" My dad said, "Watch your mouth, Big Mama. My little boy over there." Then she said, "I'm saying, how you doing, honey? Can I give him a hug?" And she gave me a hug. She then said, "He look just like his daddy. No, Johnny, he look better than you, he-he-he."

In junior high I went to parties; a little card was given out in the hallways, on the playground, during lunch, or on the street. The cards said, "Party: date, gate, rate, and mate." The rate was to get in—it might have been twenty-five to fifty cents. The gate was the address, and the mate was whoever was the host. It was always dark inside, with red and blue lights. We would hang out, smoke weed, drink, meet people, and try to get a girl. I fell in love with a girl named Alfreda Rutledge. She would always say, "Come on, Johnny. Let's slow dance." The music played on 45s: James Brown, Sam Cooke, Otis Redding, and Jackie Wilson—my guy. You would hear the Supremes, Martha Reeves and the Vandellas, and Stevie Wonder. That's what the kids in Detroit listened to. Now, my dad was a music enthusiast; he loved Marvin Gaye and James Brown. Of course, he knew the jazz musician Wes Montgomery and was friends with Jimmy Smith, the Hammond B-3 organ player, but his main concentration was blues.

At age eleven, I started smoking cigarettes. I didn't like alcohol, because it tasted terrible. I first learned about marijuana when I saw my Uncle Paul and my cousin Erma Ruth down in the basement on Jameson Street. I smelled this funny stuff and went downstairs. They said, "Go back upstairs, boy." That's when I realized marijuana was dope.

My dad used to have all his rehearsals in the basement, with the windows that were aboveground. The whole street, everybody on the block, would come around; he was the only musician in the vicinity. There was dancing in the street and partying on the side of the house.

My mother was a pretty lady, desired by many men—and she knew it. My dad was always out of town. My little brother and I were taken to Big Mama's or our cousin Erma Ruth's, or sometimes our cousin Joe would babysit us so mama could do her thing while papa was away. It broke my little heart; I grew up very angry. You could call me and Robert the drop-off kids, as we were always being dropped off somewhere. Mama was a young partier, who loved the nightlife and the attention. Sometimes, when my dad had come back from tour and she was missing in action, we'd travel down Mack Avenue, looking for her. One time, after driving and searching for many hours, we heard her yell, "Johnny, Junior, Robert!"

Robert yelled, "Daddy, there's mama."

He stopped and she jumped into the backseat. Robert and I would hug her because we'd missed her.

Beginning when I was four or five years old, a married man—a neighbor named Bo Collins, who lived about four houses down—entered our lives. He was the perpetrator who would cause my parents to divorce. What did I know as a boy? I didn't know where my mom went when she left home at night. If I went to visit Big Mama or my cousins while my dad was out, I didn't know what was going on—but I had my suspicions. I believe this was the trauma that ran my whole life down to the ground. It inspired a song I later wrote, called "Keep It Real": one of the lines says, "You can't put a Band-Aid over a bullet wound. If you don't get stitches quick, it'll bleed real soon. Keep it real." I tried to use drugs to cover the pain and agony caused by my mama cheating on my daddy. It devastated me. I grew up hating Bo Collins. When he would come around, my mother would say, "Boy, you better speak to him." But I didn't speak to him and then would be punished: I couldn't go outside or watch television.

As I sit here with tears in my eyes, I am reminded of when Jesus said, "The thief comes only to steal and kill and destroy; I have come that they may have life, and have it to the full" (John 10:10). I witnessed the devil destroy my family; the effects were evident throughout much of my life.

Later, when I was older (maybe twelve or thirteen), when my dad was out of town, I would walk past my mother's room and hear them inside together. My dad would leave, and here comes Bo Collins, like a rat that's waiting on the people to sleep so he can steal their food; that was his routine. I would get so mad I'd slam my hand on the door on my way downstairs; I knew I would get in trouble. My mother wanted respect. She would hit me with a belt over and over. I cried, not because of the pain but because of the evil it exemplified. After the beating I would yell, "I hate him!"

She'd say, "You watch your mouth, boy, or I'll whip your ass again. Now, go to your room!"

I cried in my room on my bed, saying, "I want my daddy."

At some point, when I got older, she hit me, and I grabbed the belt with one hand. I let her know how I felt. I believe if I'd been big enough, I would have beaten up or killed Bo Collins. But thank God I didn't. Here I am; I'm alive and not in prison for killing anyone. I'm a preacher of the gospel now, but that's how I used to feel.

Through my adolescence this went on: the parties, the infidelity, dad out of town, and my growing up becoming unmanageable. I stayed out all night long, sometimes knowing I would get a beating upon my return. It was worth it. Sometimes, when I'd come home late from getting high at parties, the lights were on when they should have been off. My mother and father were accusing each other of cheating, lying to each other. My dad's smoking gun was the lipstick on his white shirts; I was the eyewitness to my mother's cheating. My dad slept on the couch, or sometimes I'd come home and he would be sleeping in my bed. It was so sad—even a kid could understand there was evil in the house. The devil destroyed my mother's and father's marriage as well as most of my life, with drugs and time spent in jails and prisons.

Over and over, I was told, "You ain't going to grow up to be nothing, Junior. You will use dope the rest of your life. Somebody will kill you, or you're gonna wind up in prison for the rest of your life. Just watch and see." Upon my dad's return from overseas, he would get a report from my mother: "Junior stays out all night, and he's smoking weed. He and Robert fight all the time, and he talks back to me."

I believe my dad's guilty feelings over his infidelity and his desire to show a good face toward my mother explain his rage toward me; he would beat me with an extension cord. If Robert and I got into a fight or if I came home late while he was in town, he would go into a fit, pull his belt from his pants, and swing so hard with the belt to my back, you could hear it across the room. If he didn't have a belt, he would grab the extension cord from the iron and swing so violently it would break my flesh.

One morning, around 1:00, I was awakened by a fight between my mother and father. My mother was cursing at my dad; she had a baseball bat in her hands and was swinging. She hit my father in the side and swung again. I grabbed the bat and told her to leave him alone. She said, "Get out of the way, Junior!"

My dad came forward, trying to take the bat from her. I said, "Daddy, please leave."

As he approached, she swung again, hitting him. He fell down the stairs and fractured his left arm. At that moment, I hated my mother for injuring my father; it was like she had hit me. She feared him to a certain extent—probably because of her guilty conscience from cheating on him. She cut him on his arm as he was trying to defend himself.

After my older sisters moved out, my dad would retreat to their old room to sleep, as, at that time, my parents were estranged. My dad would smell of alcohol after returning home from a gig, but no matter what, he always remembered that if she wasn't there, the boys might be hungry. He would stop at Green's Deep South Barbeque. Like clockwork he would wake us up and ask, "Ba-ba-ba-are y'all hungry?" What a joy it is to reflect now on those nights: a loving wake-up call.

Eventually, because of the infidelity, they decided to divorce. They just couldn't get along anymore. Even after the divorce, when my dad came back from doing shows on the road, he always stayed in the house, either in my room, in Robert's room, or in my sisters' room. He always made sure there was money for bills and groceries. Despite their differences, they were putting the kids first. When my dad told me they were splitting up, it broke my heart. It's the worst thing that a child can go through. I didn't know what to do. I walked the streets and cried.

As I became more aware of the problems inside my home, I started experimenting with more drugs. I attempted to cover my problems by doing what the in-crowd was doing. As a kid, I faced double dares and peer pressure, not force—just the desire to feel part of a group and to distance myself from the reality of what was going on in my family.

Then, too, to a kid, there's always an experiment or adventure you want to try. When mothers and fathers shelter their kids, they draw a line: "You can't go over there." Then the kid becomes curious about what's on the other side. Kids put their hand in the fire to see what it feels like and stick their hands in fences to see if the dog will bite. They cross the line and find out this is what they're missing. I started to ask, "What's down the street or around the forbidden corner? What's a party like?" So I went to those places. But it's just like when God told Adam and Eve, "You may surely eat of every tree in the garden [except the middle one] . . . the day you eat of it, you will surely die" (Genesis 2:16–17). The devil comes into your mind and says, "You won't get into any trouble. God knows the day you do it, you're going to have a ball." Adam's and Eve's curiosity made them want to feel wise, like God. I wanted to see what the high felt like, so one day, Sugar Man and I put some glue into a paper bag and sniffed it. It blew our heads off. I saw stars; I had blindness. We were like zombies. We were not ourselves. It was a high that made me feel like if I did it again, I would have a heart attack and die. Trust me, I never did that again.

I graduated from sniffing glue to drinking Robitussin cough syrup with alcohol in it. To buy it legally, you had to be twenty-one or older. It cost two dollars for a four-ounce bottle. My cousin Junior Mathis and I would wait at the corner of the drugstore and ask cool-looking guys to take our money and buy us a bottle. Most consented, but some kept our money and told us, "Get lost, boy, or I'll tell yo' mama." Soon pills, marijuana, wine, and liquor were on the table. It was cool to be one of the teenagers who got high. If you weren't, you were a square and a sissy. The Robitussin would kind of relax you, making you nod and scratch your skin off, but it made you just forget about everything.

As trouble between my parents grew, my acts of rebellion increased and became more evident. I kept fading away: staying out late at night and coming home both high and angry. My mother would yell at me and demand that I accept that other woman's husband as my friend, but I wouldn't. She yelled at me when I wouldn't speak to him. If he called and asked to speak to her, I'd hang up on him. I wanted to kill Bo Collins. I was angry enough to contemplate how to get away with it: "Should I buy a pistol and ambush him one night? Or should I have my boys beat him up real bad?" Murder was a life sentence, so I quickly got rid of those evil thoughts.

Drugs shut out a lot of things; they were the Band-Aids to cover what was going on at home or for getting fired from a job. I'd tell myself, "Just get high, drink some Robitussin syrup, smoke some weed, drink some wine." After a while, I went from the four- to the eight-ounce bottle of Robitussin. I came to learn later on that while it's not like heroin, I became hooked on this syrup: I had withdrawals.

When my sisters, Diane and Zakiya, were teenagers, they were party girls. They loved to go to parties, dance, and go roller-skating. The Graystone Ballroom was their favorite place to dance with their boyfriends. They never used drugs. I don't know—maybe they tried at parties and didn't like it, but it never became a part of their lifestyles, thank God. They didn't drink wine or smoke cigarettes; I never saw them smoke weed. They were straight up squares, and that was a good thing. They never went to jail except to see me. My mother was the same: no drugs, no cigarettes, and no weed. If she did have a drink at a party, she never brought it home. My mother and father said to me, "We don't do none of this stuff. How did you become a dope addict?" My family had no understanding of the causes: the peer pressure, my hanging with the wrong people, and the type of stress I was going through. My mother would tell my dad, "I think Junior's taking something." One night I came in late when my dad was home, and he hit me so hard that I had welts on my back and across my shoulders. But the whippings weren't going to do anything, especially when I was hooked on drugs; it was my heart that needed to be changed. The scriptures say, "The heart is deceitful above all things and desperately wicked, who can know it?" (Jeremiah 17:9).

While we were living on Jameson Street, my father got Robert and me a Hammond B-3 organ for Christmas. He paid Bob Thurman, his keyboard player, to teach us to play. Robert caught on right away. I still remember the first lesson, but I never really connected with it in the way Robert did. His whole family, including his daughters and his son, all play. Robert, of course, played with Van Morrison and my dad on *I'll Never Get Out of These Blues Alive*. I took lessons, but the things going on around us affected me more than the others. I don't know why, only God knows. I tried guitar, too, but I didn't stick with it. I ventured off into drugs.

When I was about thirteen, I entered a singing contest at the Fox Theater. The first prize was $500 and a contract to get into Motown.

My dad was out of town, so he couldn't play guitar with me. His first call was to Jimmy Reed, but he was incapacitated—in other words, he was drunk. My dad then asked Eddie Taylor to take me and my mother downtown to the Fox. My dad probably paid him fifty dollars to back me, but I still lost.

At about the same time, I had a vocal group in the neighborhood. I was inspired by my dad and wanted to be a recording star. Larry and Jerry Geter, Sugar Man, and Tony Pollard were in the group. They are all dead now. We sang covers. We all had a crush on this lady who went by the name of Bonnie and was twenty years older than us. We'd go on the side of her house and sing, "Oh, oh, oh, oh, oh, oh, Bonnie, you belong to me." We couldn't harmonize; but we were trying to imitate the Motown sound. I was the lead singer.

One day, my mother made an appointment and took me and Larry Geter downtown to West Grand Boulevard to Motown Records, "Hitsville, USA." A man came down for the audition to see what kind of talent we had. When we walked in, he said, "Let me see what you got." We began to sing. Now that I'm a grown man, I can see that he didn't want to break our hearts. He asked, "What grade are you in?" I told him what grade, and he said, "When you finish high school, come back and talk to me." That was his kind way of saying, "You're not ready, kids."

Even with all the destruction going on in my life, looking back, I'd say some of my favorite memories are from when my three baby sisters were born: Shyvonne, Lavetta, and Karen. Shyvonne was a dancer, Karen was the spoiled one, and Lavetta liked school. As a ruthless dope fiend, I stole from them. I tricked Karen and stole her Atari, making her cry. I tricked Shyvonne and ran out the door with her typewriter. And I stole Lavetta's first color TV. Lavetta was the tough kid. She'd fight anybody. One day, I robbed a dope dealer's flunky. They caught up with me maybe a week later, while I was making a call in a phone booth, and started beating me up. Somebody told Lavetta. She ran down there and told them to get off her brother, and they stopped: Lavetta to the rescue!

My dad was a struggling musician for a while. He worked hard, and nobody could tell him he wasn't going to become successful one day. With "Boogie Chillen" and "Boom Boom," he was recognized for his authenticity and his rawness. He was no copycat; he was an original.

But he didn't make a lot of money. The house we rented was in bad shape: we had roaches galore—so many that when you turned on the lights after being away from home, you could hear them crawling. My dad did everything he could to keep the lights on. Sometimes he was late with payments, though, and our heat and electricity were cut off. We had to light candles to see our way through the house. When the electricity was off, my mother would call cousin Willie to secretly turn it back on. He'd climb up the pole, and when he came down, the lights were on, but we had to turn them off at night so we wouldn't get caught cheating.

We had a furnace in the basement for which a truck would dump coal through the window and onto the floor, and then we'd have to shovel it in. Sometimes we'd have to sleep in our clothes and wrap up with extra blankets when the coal bill was not paid on time. When dad did finally get paid, he'd send my mother money through Western Union for groceries and bills. My mother would pay the light bill and buy groceries and school clothes, and we'd each get two dollars to go to the movies (it only cost fifty cents back then).

My dad had to record under different names because some people in the industry tried to trick him out of royalties. Some got away with it, but he caught on. He was illiterate and couldn't read his contracts, so he had his closest friends read them to him. When we lived together in California, he would ask me to read and tell him what the advance and final payment were. I'd let him know, and he would sign with his own unique signature. My dad was cheated out of thousands of dollars, if not millions, because he could not read or write, but God was with him. He finally got some of the money he was owed in the late 1980s.[1] Just like the Jeffersons, he "moved on up" and "finally got a piece of the pie." From that point on, he had attorneys. He always told me, "Before you sign a contract, make sure you read and understand. Don't shake hands. I don't care if your brother is your producer, you don't sign. Make sure you have an attorney, a manager. Tell them to let you see the paperwork and documentation first. If they do not have that along with an advance, Junior, do not do it. You hear me?"

When we didn't have money or his car wasn't working and was in the shop, my dad would walk down the street like the other fathers, headed toward McClellan Street to catch the Department of Street Railways (DSR) bus to the Apex Bar or the 20 Grand Ballroom. Sometimes he asked me to loan him ten dollars until the next day; I was so happy to loan my dad some money. It gave me the feeling that I was paying him back for all the love he had shown all of us. He always paid me back. I remember two particular occasions when I loaned him bus fare. I never caught the bus with him, but I was so proud to carry his guitar. It makes me cry to think about it now.

Because of his hit record "Boogie Chillen," my dad was able to move up the ladder a little and rent a house instead of an apartment or a "one-room country shack," as he would say. Later, promoters from Europe started calling on John Lee Hooker to perform. My dad got busy; he was over the hump at last.

I continued experimenting with drugs and tried cocaine. Some people like to use it just to stay up all day, but not me. One solution was to take cocaine to pick me up and then drink some cough syrup to come back down. But if I got some good cocaine, I had to drink a lot of cough syrup, and that wasn't cool. During that time, I also took prescription sedatives, like Tuinal and Secos, or red devils. My drug addiction progressed. I was taking two of this and three of that, trying to mellow myself down.

I started hanging out with a couple of dudes named Dennis Bates and Jerry Murphy, who were a little older than me and a little more street savvy. One day, Dennis put some lines on the table and said, "Try this." Heroin only cost one or two dollars back in those days, and it came in gelatin caps. In Detroit, heroin was cut with quinine and lactose; when you snorted it, it burned your nose. If you continued to do it, sometimes the cocaine and the heroin would make your nose bleed and give you uncomfortable vision. And if you caught a cold, you'd sneeze fluids and blood. There had to be a better way: I saw a guy who was shooting dope, and he explained, "Do it this way. It'll go to your head and get you high quicker. You won't get that nasty, terrible drain in your mouth." So I started shooting dope in my hands, as the veins hadn't developed in my arms yet—I was still a young boy. I shot dope throughout the week, day in and day out. My hands began to swell up like boxing gloves because I would sometimes miss the vein and it would just go anywhere in the tissue of my hands.

I witnessed some of the fiends shooting dope into their neck and groin. After they'd burnt out all their easily accessed veins, every time they wanted to get high, they had to drop their pants to find a vein. Even some of the women in the shooting galleries would do the same.

I prayed I would never have to do that; it was horrible. But this was the horrible life I had chosen, right? I saw one guy shooting dope in a vein in his head—an experiment I have learned to hate. And I saw the destruction it caused not only in my life but also in my cousin Shirley's and her brother Junior's lives. He died in prison, and she died in the hospital. At the time, I wouldn't say, "Oh my God," realizing it could happen to me. While Junior or someone else was shooting dope in their groin, I would think, "I sure hope I don't have to go through that," but there was also this haunting realization: "You're on your way."

The stealing progressed with the drugs. When I was a kid, I used to watch *The Untouchables*, the *Purple Gang*, and *Black Bart*—all kinds of shows about crime. I don't blame the TV, but it could have been an influence on my behavior. As a kid, I wanted more and more. Miss Nettie had a store on the corner of Jameson Street, and Mr. Jones had one on Charlevoix Street, on the way to the junior high. If I didn't have money, I would do like the other kids and steal little stuff. It's like the scriptures say, "The little foxes ruin the vineyards" (Song of Songs 2:15), and as Jesus said, "A little yeast works through the whole batch of dough" (Galatians 5:9): a little evil corrupts everything. The stealing led to more. Money just intrigued me, like with the Boy Scouts or the shoe flap in church. I watched and learned, but I was also greedy. "Yet man is born to trouble as surely as sparks fly upward" (Job 5:7). Every person is born into this world with a corrupt nature. No one had to teach me how to be bad. It just developed because of what I saw, what I needed, and what I could get. I developed into a low-down thug, a thief, and eventually a con player. I was in a dog-eat-dog way, and it didn't matter if you were my family. The pin-striped suits, the hand-stitched gabardine shirts with the collars up, and the alligators all demonstrated back in the day that you were a player, but all that hip stuff was about to disappear; I had become a monster. With the drugs it was easy enough to continue stealing. Today I look back as a Christian and say, "Boy, I was a big dummy." It was all vanity and vainglory, just enough to send me to hell. If not for the grace and mercy of God, I'd be in prison for the rest of my life.

My parents knew something was wrong. I was losing jobs and being accused of stealing. When I was around fourteen or fifteen, a friend and I were caught trying to break into a boat at Belle Isle. I think we'd gotten away with a portable TV. I don't know if the boat had an alarm, but as soon as we left, there were flashlights and loud voices saying, "Don't move." They took us to juvenile hall and tricked us into telling on each other. An officer came in and said, "You might as well tell the truth, 'cause your friend said you did it."

I said, "No, I didn't. He did it."

The officer answered, "Well, tell me what happened."

Then I explained, "When we went there, blah, blah, blah . . ."

We both sang like canaries in a cage.

When I was taken to juvenile hall, my mother was at work, and my dad was out of town. My mother's boyfriend, Bo, came and told me, "Junior, your mother's so worried about you and don't know what to do. She just wants to know what's going on with you."

I was having withdrawals, so I told him I was addicted to heroin. I really didn't want to talk to him. I told him to tell her I'd be alright, that I was getting cleaned up in there. I withdrew cold turkey. After a while, maybe two or three weeks, the judge agreed to allow my parents to take me home. I was given house arrest and probation. When my dad came home, he asked, "What's wrong with you, man?"

I said, "I'm hooked on heroin," but they didn't understand. They said they'd never used drugs and asked me to stop. I really wanted to stop. But there's something about addiction. It leaves an indentation inside of your mind and controls you. Physically, your craving comes from the aches, pains, vomiting, sweats, and migraine headaches, but spiritually, addiction is demonically driven. One time, when I was a boy, I stole a color TV out of the back of a pickup. I took the TV, walked down the street, crossed over, and a grown man stopped me: "Don't you make another step." He took the TV out of my hands and beat me down to the ground; he almost killed me. The devil showed me what it would look like if I got away: I saw a picture of victory. But the devil doesn't tell you about consequences. That's what happened most of my life: consequences caught up with me. The only way I was able to get rid of the power of drugs was by the power of God.

I hated myself, and I would often tell myself I could quit. But I often remembered how it felt the first time I'd taken a hit of heroin, and I wanted to recapture that same feeling. I lied to myself: "I'm just going to do it one time, feel good, and then I ain't going to mess with it no more." You lie to yourself, but you're back, hooked again. I had a loving family that believed I could do better, but I was no good to the core. I could actually look into a mirror and acknowledge that to myself. I knew if I didn't get off dope, I would die someday—and maybe soon.

# 3

# HEROIN, PROSTITUTES, AND FIRST ARREST AS AN ADULT

There was a lot of racial unrest in Detroit; for lack of a better word, it was anarchy. We read about it in the news, heard about it on the radio and through the grapevine, and witnessed it: racial profiling, crooked police, gambling on street corners, after-hour joints galore, and dope houses springing up like 7-Elevens. There were murders on this side of town and big drug busts on that side of town. There was constant racial conflict, and finally, somebody just got fed up. I don't know who started it; all I know is what my dad wrote in a song called "The Motor City Is Burning." The newspapers also said it started on Twelfth Street and Clairmount Avenue. It didn't just explode all in that one day—July 23, 1967. It was a process, and it got really big. All through the morning and in the afternoon, it just got bigger. We lived on the east side and saw the smoke in the air coming from the west side. That is exactly what my dad wrote about: fire engines and people shooting at firemen and throwing rocks, like in protests today. The riots spread; people joined in. They burned down a shoe store on the corner of Mack Avenue and McClellan Street and broke into drug stores, and some broke into banks, stealing even the nickels, dimes, and pennies. The looting was televised on channels two and seven, but everyone on the block was sitting on the front porch, watching the smoke from the fires and listening to the sirens.

My dad told me, "Junior, you stay away from there because they killing people; folks going to jail." As a rebellious, drug-addicted teenager, I wasn't hearing it. That's just like saying, "Don't use no more dope today, John." My mind was racing and scheming at the same time. Hardheaded me, I went out the door and toward the action. I stopped by Miss Nettie's store first and saw how they had rummaged the place. They'd stolen everything that poor old woman had worked her whole life to earn. I loved Miss Nettie, and she never reopened. I got to the corner of Mack Avenue and McClellan Street, crossed, and noticed they were robbing Cunningham's Drug Store, so I joined in the looting. I walked in the broken entrance of that store hoping to get drugs, but they were cleaned out. I was disappointed but started grabbing what I could—anything of value—and headed out the door with my arms full of stolen property.

As I came out of the store, I headed to the fence man's house three blocks away to sell the stolen goods and was approached by a fat White police officer. His face looked as though he was in a panic, scared for his life. His gun was drawn and, without warning, he shot toward my upper body, trying to kill me; I heard the bullet pass by my head. I didn't drop the goods but ran in the opposite direction, and ironically, so did he. It was very dangerous on Mack Avenue; people were getting killed. I think that if he had killed me, he would've gotten away with murder. Black lives didn't matter on that day.

The story of the riot was all over the local and national news, maybe even going global. A journalist would think, "This is news. I better get my camera and note pad." My dad said, "I'm going to the studio to record." In September 1967 he came out with a charted single, "The Motor City Is Burning." It was fresh off the stove, as it were: "Oh, the Motor City is burning, people. There is nothing in the world that I can do. Well, it started on Twelfth and Clairmount this morning, fire wagons everywhere. . . . Takin' my wife and my family, and little Johnny Lee is clearing out." Even after the song came out, the residue of the riot was lingering: the cops were still making arrests. It didn't just stop with everybody going home. No, it was still going on, and he hit it. My dad was a true storyteller, and all his ideas came from his experience and life in general.

I was able to graduate from Foch Junior High in 1968 because two smart girls named Marcia Ball and Greta Berry always helped me cheat on tests. I'd slide my paper over to them, and they'd slide theirs to me. It was easy to cheat back then—these days, you'd be in big trouble. So that's how I graduated from junior high and went on to Southeastern

High School. Going to school at Southeastern was hit or miss. I skipped to get high and to plan how to hit the next lick or crime. Pickpocketing was one of my main things, especially during recess or lunchtime. I got into many fights—most of the time, I'd started them. Sometimes a bully would want to test me, like when Michael Woods tried to bully Greta Berry in class one day. I beat him and got suspended. But everything in high school was brief; I was on my way out.

Drugs will blind you; they will take over your mind-set. You become a robot for the devil. People overdose, and you step over the body just so you can get well. It's an ice-cold feeling: all you want to do is hustle, steal, and rob somebody, no matter who it is. If it was a family member, I'd think, "I'll apologize later. I'll pay you back later. But, right now, I got to do this." When I saw my mother, I didn't think, "She birthed me from the womb and took care of me." And no drug addict can tell me, "I had integrity as a drug addict, I didn't do those evil things." They may not have done some of the evil and low things I did, but they did something.

My answer to the passive dope fiend who has a bank account, a job, and a family is as follows: "Maybe your bones didn't hurt. Maybe your eyes didn't feel like they were about to fall out of your head. Or maybe you weren't so sick that you pooped on yourself if you walked too fast. I'm happy for you that you didn't get as dirty as others and I did. More power to you, but know that it was by God's grace and mercy—and not anything that you did."

Trust me, drugs will make you crazy. They numb you so you have no respect for yourself or those around you, not even the police. There is no fear; you're oblivious to death. Heroin dealers named their packages. If somebody overdosed on a package called Murder One, that's what we wanted—the one that killed the person, the drugs that killed Greta Berry (yes, the one who'd helped me cheat) or her brother June Bug. Everybody's overdosing, and you just don't care. You say to yourself, "If I die, this is how I want to go: high as a kite on a windy day."

I know people reading this are going to say, "You were a cold, low-life thug. You were a raving wolfdog." I know I was; I was a slick snake in the grass. Al Wilson recorded a song called "The Snake," which is about a half-frozen snake that a kind woman sees and decides to take home with her.[1] After she takes care of him and he thaws, he bites her. When she asks why he did it, the snake replies, "You knew darn well that I was a snake before you took me in." I was that snake, level with the ground.

---

On my sixteenth birthday, my father bought me a car, a 1962 Catalina, so I could go to school and get a job. I got a job at a factory in Dearborn and was fired within a week for being missing in action. It was easier to drive other hustlers; I took dope dealers to the west side to pick up their packages; burglars, to hit their licks; and users, to cop their dope. My Catalina was a magnet; it attracted burglars, dope fiends, robbers, prostitutes, and the scum of the streets.

My Catalina and my name were now "reputable" on Kercheval Street at the poolroom. I even attracted the infamous, late NBA basketball star and dope fiend Reginald Harding, who had once played for the Chicago Bulls and the Detroit Pistons. He'd played with Wilt Chamberlain. I would often see Reggie inside the galleries shooting or buying dope. One day, he said, "Let's go hit a lick, youngster," and I agreed. He couldn't go inside stores to shoplift, because he was just about seven feet tall. So he would lift me up on his shoulders to the second-floor windows that were open. If the windows weren't open, we'd break them. Then I would crawl through and come back downstairs to open the door for him. We would steal TVs, typewriters, cameras, and machinery, then head over to the fence man's spot. This went on for quite some time until I realized this dude was a maniac.

Reggie Harding was a bully. I learned that he'd raped Florence Ballard of the Supremes, who then became so depressed after the ordeal that she lost her spot with the famous group. It was so sad. He got so dirty that he started robbing the dope houses and dope fiends too. One day, I was sitting in a dope house, and the word was out: Reggie had robbed the dope house of the notorious John Clackson, and there was a hit out on him. They were looking for him. A knock would come at the door of a shooting gallery; a man would pull the rifle out and aim at the top of the door because they knew he was tall. I cut Reggie loose; he was bad news.

One early morning around two o'clock, after I finished shooting my dope, I was walking downstairs when somebody grabbed me around the neck and said, "Don't move, Bam Bam. I don't want to hurt you, boy." Reggie choked me a little bit more. He could have killed me and thrown me under the stairs; nobody would've known or cared. I had just made forty dollars and only spent twenty of it, so he went in my pocket and stole those four five-dollar bills. I was so hurt; I think I started crying because I couldn't defend myself. I hated him for that and would never forget it. He then robbed a pimp and dope dealer named Slim. Slim's people caught up to him and broke his kneecaps. The next time I saw Reggie, he was rolling around Kercheval Street in a wheelchair, asking for handouts. Nobody felt sorry for him. After I left Detroit, Reggie was killed on Parkview Drive, across the street from the place owned by my cousins Dennis and Richard. Someone had shot him twice in the head.[2]

When I was sixteen, I used to drive around with an older boy, a dropout named Dennis. He had big lips and tiny eyes, and he literally talked out of the side of his mouth—like a gangster, like Edward G. Robinson or James Cagney. He was a robber, too, and always carried a gun. We went on licks together, drinking cough syrup, smoking weed, and shooting dope. One day, after we had just done some drugs, Dennis said his mother's house had been broken into and he wanted to find the suspect his mother had identified: a guy named Pie. I drove Dennis and another guy to the pool hall and waited outside. They went in, and when they came back out, they had Pie between them, with a gun to his back. Dennis hit Pie upside his head with the pistol and threw him in the backseat. Then he turned the gun on me and told me to drive. Pie was in the backseat, crying and begging for his life. When we got to his mother's house, Dennis and his partner pulled the boy out of the backseat, and we all went in the front door. Dennis's mother was there, saying, "Dennis, no! Don't do that, please."

He said, "I got this, Mama. Don't worry about it. Ain't nothin's gonna happen."

His mother pleaded, "Please don't hurt that boy, Dennis. Just call the police."

"Calm down, Mama. I got this," he answered.

We all went down to the basement, they tied Pie to a metal pole, and they beat and kicked him while burning him with cigarettes. I went into a panic. I believed I was going to witness a murder; I was also instrumental in Pie's kidnapping. They tried to calm me and tell me it would be alright. Then they just turned around and went back to beating him and burning him with cigarettes. They eventually made Pie admit he had broken into the house and tell them where the stolen goods were. He was bloody. Finally, Dennis told me, "Go on, man. Don't tell nobody." I went home, afraid they would kill him. I was getting ready to spend the rest of my life in prison. Later I found out they'd let him go. He went to the hospital. When I saw him months later, the swelling had gone down. Somehow, Pie didn't hold it against me. He later died of a heroin overdose.

I attended school every now and then. If I went, I was loaded; if I didn't go, I was out hustling or hanging out. When you're on dope, you focus on how you feel in your body and not in your brain. My dad would say to me, "I didn't have a chance to go to school. My mother and father divorced, and I had to take care of them. We were on the farm, and I had to leave because there wasn't no money there." He ran away to Memphis, and he became a theater usher and played his guitar on corners; the rest is history. He would say, "Junior, you got a chance at life." It went in one ear and out the other; he would just shake his head at me in disgust.

Drugs will make you steal from your mother, father, sisters, and brother. My mother and sisters used to have to go to the bathroom with their purses under their arms. I had gotten to the point that I was a monster; I didn't even like myself. Trusted friends, neighbors, and family—no one was safe. I went next door while my neighbors went fishing, broke into their house, and took their rifles and guns. I came back loaded and nodded off while watching television. Somebody walked in and kicked my feet: "Junior, where's our rifles?" It was the neighbor next door.

I answered, "What are you talking about?"

He looked in a couple of closets but didn't want to do too much; this was my mother and father's house. He just said, "I oughta shoot you, Junior," then walked out saying, "One day, you're going to die on that dope or spend the rest of your life in prison." The neighbor's family forgave me years later, after we were all adults and my life had changed. One of them even came to a concert of mine in Ann Arbor, Michigan. He didn't say, "Remember when you broke into our house?" We're all friends to this day.

A guy who lived across the street was a little bit older than me, and he had a job making good money. One day, he invited me in to smoke some weed, wanting to get to know me. While we were in his apartment, he told me he was doing alright and pulled out a beautiful silver gun with a pearl handle. I admired and wanted it. I said, "You are so cool. Can I see it?"

He handed it over. "Be careful, man. It's loaded."

I took the gun, made sure it was loaded, pointed it at him, and said, "Get back, or I'll blow your head off."

"Man, don't do this to me," he pleaded.

I told him to sit down: "You come out this door, and I'm going to blow your brains out."

The next day, the guy saw me walking down Mack Avenue toward the dope house. He was in a car with some other people. I couldn't run, so I motioned toward my pants, where the gun was, and said, "Come on." They didn't bother me. I finally made it to the fence's house. After all that ducking and dodging, I think I sold the gun for sixty dollars. I got so high all that day and was up all night. The next day, it was time to go home. That's how dumb I was. The guy saw me and came across the street. He must have been watching and waiting on me. Who robs the guy across the street and then returns to the scene of the crime? Oblivious dope fiends do. He ran over with a big knife and said, "Give me my gun." Big Mama was sitting on the front porch. I looked at him. I don't know where my courage came from, but I challenged him: "You ain't going to do nothing with that knife." Big Mama ran out the door past him and gave me a butcher knife bigger than the one he had. Even without the butcher knife, I was stupidly unafraid. He backed off and left to go back to his apartment building.

The fire of destruction was burning a little bit hotter now; I was a little older and much more daring. I was still in my teens, but I kept coming home late and in terrible shape. My mother had had enough. She told me, "If any money come up missing from this house again, I'm going to shoot you, Junior. The next time you come in here late at night, you go find you a new place to live."

I can still see her face. "You want to be grown. The next time you come in here after curfew, you can't come back. I mean it. You hear me?" Then I came home in the wee hours of the morning, having stayed out all night, and knocked on the door. In her hands she had my lavender alpaca sweater and a pair of lavender pants, fresh out of the cleaner. She stuck them out the door and said, "Get out of here, and don't come back." Saddened, I took my pants and sweater and headed toward Mack Avenue. I sold the two-piece outfit, and I went and got high.

The same thing that almost got me killed, sent me to jail, and made my family reject me—I went right back to it: dope. My mother wasn't bluffing. I was not allowed to come back to her home, but my sister Zakiya and her late husband, Glenn, lived upstairs. They took me in and allowed me to sleep on their couch. After I burned that bridge, Big Mama allowed me to sleep across the bottom of her bed, in her very small studio. The scriptures say, "Good judgment wins favor, but the way of the unfaithful leads to their destruction" (Proverbs 13:15).

# CHAPTER 3

The life of any dope fiend is hard; you have to feed the gorilla that's on your back—or die. Stealing prescription pads from a doctor's office and selling the pills, stealing checks from a mailbox and selling them to a forger—you do whatever it takes. I became a vulture: I did anything I could to get dope. I often confessed to myself that I was a loser and would soon die.

I used to hustle with a guy named Jaymo, who introduced me to the pimp, Garland, he worked for. Garland had three prostitutes working upstairs from a shoe store. After a quick interview, Garland hired me. His instructions were brief: "You watch my girls. You make sure none of these tricks don't do nothing to 'em. You understand? You make twenty, twenty-five dollars a night. If it's a good night, I might give you a little bit more." This seemed cool because I could still hustle in the daytime.

Jaymo and I took turns: while one watched out to make sure the tricks didn't hurt any of the girls and paid for the product, the other one guarded the cars. We were supposed to make sure the mark got in his car safely and drove off so he might return someday. But the tricks were always thinking, "I better leave my money and jewelry in my car, because she might get me," and we knew that. The prostitutes would signal to us if the guy didn't have his wallet, and we would break into the car. The pimp didn't like that. Garland wanted to make sure the tricks came back as regular customers, but we got diamond watches, diamond rings, and wads of money. Cadillacs had a button in the glove compartment to pop the trunk open. That's what Jaymo and I would do.

Another "job" was stealing from the tricks in the room. If they were from another country, cheating on their wife, or a White or Chinese guy, they always kept their pants and shoes on while they were having sex—smart, but we were one step ahead of them. The women exaggerated their noises and shook the bed really hard; I would creep in while they were distracted. With their pants around their ankles, I would tap the pocket. If the wallet was there, I would unbutton it, pull the wallet out, step outside into the hallway, take the money, creep back, and put the wallet back in his pants. Keep in mind, the trick always paid up front, before he received his product. We made a deal with the ladies: if they didn't tell Garland, we'd split the money with them.

I was making money; it all went right back into my arm: I got high every night. We didn't care about Garland's business flourishing. We cared about our habit. But there were too many complaints from the tricks about their cars being broken into, jewelry stolen, and money missing. They said it wasn't safe for them to come back. One time, when some valuable items came up missing, Garland sent out a threat to kill us if the diamond watch and color TV weren't returned. He would pay any dope fiend to stick us. I must admit I was scared. I didn't know where to go—I was a four-corner hustler between Mack Avenue and Kercheval Street. The watch was sold and shot up into our arms; however, we returned the TV as a "peace offering." It inflated Garland's ego when we showed up with the stolen property. It also kept his reputation on the streets as a gangster pimp. He was happy to receive the TV as a sign that his threat had worked. He said, "I oughta have both y'all taken care of, but I'ma let you live. But you fired. Don't come around my spot ever again."

I never saw Jaymo again. I went on to shooting dice in allies, gambling shacks, and abandoned houses, as well as continuing to commit burglaries and steal checks. I hustled pool at the spot across the street from the prostitute house. I wouldn't mess with the best pool sharks, but sometimes I would pretend to be drunk and bet somebody who thought I couldn't play. I'd hold my stick a certain way, make a bet, and then beat them. Sometimes I plain beat out somebody because I knew how to bank the balls really well—not bad for a junkie teenager. Upstairs from the poolroom was the dope house owned and operated by a dealer named Eddie Seals, who was shot to death on Kercheval Street. They sold dollar caps of China white heroin, which killed many of the people I knew, if not by overdose, then by abscesses on their necks, legs, or hands.

One night out on Mack Avenue, I was casing cars, tricks, and houses to see if I could get some dope before I became sick. I stopped by the house of a man named Big Bo and approached the door with a burglar tool in my back pocket. I knocked on the door, the door opened, and *boom*! I don't remember anything; I was knocked out cold. At the time, I was seventeen years old and only about 135 lbs. of skin and bones, from using dope. The next thing I knew, I was looking up into a bright light and lying on a hard wooden bench. I used my left hand to prop up and grabbed a bar to raise myself. I was in jail at 1300 Beaubien Street in downtown Detroit, with both my eyes swollen shut. My face felt like a puffed-up basketball. My lips were fat, and I tasted blood. When I woke up, the guard called, "Hooker, let's go. You're being released. No charges have been filed." He went on to say someone was there to pick me up. I could barely walk straight; I couldn't see, and the pain was excruciating. The same person who'd kicked me out of the house and told me never to come back was there to pick me up: my mother.

My sisters' friend Cynthia lived across the street from Big Bo and recognized me as Diane's and Zakiya's brother. She'd heard the ruckus and seen what was going on. Because she knew how violent Bo could be, she called the police. She also called my mother—my dad was out on the road—and told her Big Bo was beating me up. I was unconscious on the porch, and he was telling someone to hurry up with boiling water so he could pour it on me and scald my face. Bo's excuse for knocking me out was that I was a drug addict and had a screwdriver in my back pocket. He probably told the police, "Look at his hands, he's a dope fiend. He was going to break into my house." No charges were filed against Big Bo. When I walked out of the jail, my mother looked at me with horror in her eyes and said, "Junior, look at you. What have you done, boy?"

I was speechless and ashamed as she led me to her car by the arm, making sure I didn't fall. I wished I could either die or disappear. "Where are we going?" I asked.

She said, "I am taking you home, Junior." With all I'd put her through, here was a mother's love.

Tears ran down my face, but she couldn't see them; my face was a mess of blood, dirt, and sweat. My mother told me I wasn't dead because Cynthia had called the police. It's by the grace of God that I didn't have a concussion or a disfigured face from the boiling water Big Bo planned to pour on me.

I told myself I would wait awhile, go back, and kill Big Bo for what he'd done. But realizing that he'd acted out of wrath against me for what I was about to do to his house, I let it go. My mother and my little sisters Shyvonne and Lavetta nursed me back to health. After one month in the house, my mother warned me, "If you go back out there and keep doing what you're doing, somebody is gonna kill you, Junior. Don't come back here if you do." But I was back on the streets, robbing, stealing, and doing dope—exactly as the scriptures say: "As a dog returns to its vomit, so fools repeat their folly" (Proverbs 26:11).

One day, I sold the fence man some stolen regular typewriters. He asked if I could get any IBM ball typewriters. I knew exactly where to get some. I walked into my old school, Foch Junior High School, during recess; went into the empty typing classroom; and unlocked the window to come back later. That night, I knew I had to get in and out quickly, before the alarm above the window seal went off. I opened the window and lowered down two typewriters by the cord so they wouldn't just crash on the ground. I carried them to my car, threw them in the backseat, and got away. I took them straight to the fence man. I got a lot of money, maybe eighty or a hundred dollars. I remember those twenties looked so nice. Then I was on my way to get dollar caps of heroin. I bought ten and stayed high for three or four days. The police—the lawless Big Four—were on the take: the fence man was giving them stolen goods so he wouldn't go to jail.

When my money ran out, the fence asked big-dummy me if I could get more; he had some special customers who'd ordered them. I waited a while and went back to the same school, unlocked the same window, and let the typewriters down by the cord. The police waited for me to climb out the window and shut it, and then—the flashlights. A loud voice said, "Don't move." That was one of the saddest days of my life. I'd broken into my own school, not once but twice, through the same window. Who does that? I felt I was in big trouble this time.

# 4

# WAYNE COUNTY JAIL

The police took me downtown to 1300 Beaubien Street—again. I was processed and sent to Wayne County Jail. At seventeen, I was on the fourth floor in a cell block filled with older men, with the exception of two other youngsters: one was a pet flunky for a convict named Big John—he washed his underwear and his back while they were in the shower together—and the other was Henry. It seemed to me most of the inmates had been in and out of prison much of their lives; they loved telling war stories about the time they'd spent in there. My cell partner's name was Slim Goody. He was an older convict who took a liking to me. He stuttered, "Wh-what's your name?"

I said, "Johnny Lee Hooker Jr."

He talked real fast: "Is yo daddy's name John Lee Hooker, the famous blues singer?"

I said, "Yeah."

He said, "My mama and daddy love that man."

Slim Goody was from Mississippi, a very quiet and nice guy, but I got the sense he was a dangerous man. I learned he was without family or anyone to look out for him. As time went on, he looked at me as a little brother. He used to tell me, "Boy, you're going to 'Gladiator School' [Ionia Prison].[1] I got to get you ready." We would box; he trapped me in the corner, saying, "Come on out." I'd get so mad, I'd box my way out. We did calisthenics every day. I'm over seventy now and still do them. Every day he said, "It's time to get you ready. Let's work. Got to get you prepared, boy." Everyone respected Slim Goody and knew not to mess with him. He never tied his shoes so he would be ready to fight if needed. I remember throughout the four months we were there together, he walked on the back of his boots, except when he went to court—then he tied them up. The scriptures say, "Be aware that you're not entertaining an angel" (Hebrews 13:2). An angel can take any form it wants. Angels fight for you. I don't know, maybe Slim Goody was my guardian angel.

One night in the late hours, we heard some violent movement; the next day, everybody wanted to know what had happened. We learned that Shorty, an inmate, raped Henry. It reminded me of the time when I was about fourteen, when my mother was raped one night while coming home by herself. I remember one of my sisters woke me and told me she was in the hospital. She stayed in the hospital for a couple of days. That was one of the many traumatic things in my life. Now Shorty had raped Henry. He preyed on young, frightened people he could bluff. He'd been to Jackson and Ionia prisons.[2] We, the young guys, usually met up and talked, but the next day, I didn't see Henry. They'd moved him out of the tank, but they hadn't moved Shorty. I went to court and passed Henry as we each headed into different courtrooms. I called to him, wishing I could go over and give him a hug or help him. I asked, "What happened?" He just nodded and made a face. He didn't really have to say what had happened. I motioned with my mouth, "Shorty?" He nodded his head, "Yeah." It really upset me; this was unprecedented in my young life: a man raping another man.

The next day, Slim Goody went to court, leaving me alone in the cell, and Shorty came to my cell with a single-edge razor blade. I was doing something when he grabbed me by the shirt at the chest and said, "Don't move, boy." Instantly, I grabbed him by the neck and leg at the same time and hit him several times. He had a weapon, but I was oblivious to that; protecting myself meant everything. He must have put the razor back in his pocket; I would remember if the razor had hit the floor. He didn't want an attempted murder. His plan was to come in and intimidate me. But I was so strong; I threw him up on the top bunk, where Goody slept, and choked him. I said to myself, "I oughta kill him!"—just that quick. I thought, "If I kill him, I'll get away with it because he tried to molest me." I had him so tightly around his neck, but instinct stopped me from killing him. I had never killed anybody. I give the glory to God; I let him back down.

He said, "I was just kidding with you, youngster."

I answered, "No, you wasn't. You come in my cell again, I will kill you, Shorty."

He thought he was going to do the same thing to me that he'd done to Henry. The next day, after they had finished their investigation, they called Shorty to "roll 'em up." Everybody on the cell block knew why they told him to "roll 'em up." He was charged with rape and sent to the hole.

Time went on, and we'd hear the lyrics on the radio, "Mary Hill used to hang out in Cherry Hill Park."[3] And sometimes, guess what else would come on? "Boom, boom, boom, boom."

The guys said, "Boy, that's your daddy, boy."

Talk about *homesick*! It made me think, "Oh God, Dad, where are you?"

A new guy came in to fill the empty bunk that had belonged to Shorty. I sort of welcomed him to the tank, and we hit it off. We started talking about our charges, and the subject of drugs came up. He said his brother was going to send him some dope; I got really excited. After they'd called his name a few days later to sign for his package, he came to my cell with some shoes. We opened one heel, and there was the syringe and heroin. We got so high that we both almost overdosed. Big John, the tank bully, heard about it and got jealous. He moved the youngster out of his cell, moved the dope guy in, and turned him against me, as though I had played him. One morning I got my breakfast and headed to the table to eat. The dope guy walked up to me—and *boom!*—he hit me. It knocked the bowl of oatmeal out of my hand onto the floor. I shook it off. Then Slim Goody said, "Get him. Kick his ass."

I gave him a boxing lesson. I pulled him into my cell so the guards wouldn't see, and I whupped that full-grown man. I got him down on the bunk, and right next to me was a razor in a holder. If I'd wanted, I could have grabbed that thing. Thank you, Lord Jesus, I didn't, because I would've killed him, especially if I'd hit him in the temple in the soft spot or if I'd stabbed him in the eye. But I just beat him up.

Slim broke it up: "Big John, you're the one started this sh—. Fight me. I'm a man. That's a boy."

Everybody backed up because Slim had a bucket and mop ringer in his hand, and he was ready to kill somebody. I stood next to Slim.

The guards came in and told the one who'd hit me, "Get your stuff."

The next day, I heard, "Hooker, you got a visit."

My mother came to visit. When she saw that I had a big swollen lip, she said, "What happened to you, boy?"

I said, "I had a fight. He just came up to me and hit me."

She asked, "I know you fought him back, didn't you?"

"Yup. I whupped him," I said. "But you know what? I don't think I like this tank. My cellie is leaving for state prison tomorrow, and all of the youngsters 'cept me is either gone home or to prison. But I'll be alright. Don't worry about me."

My mother said, "I'm getting you out of there, where you can be around people your own age."

There was a guy that lived on the corner of Jameson and McClellan Streets. I remembered him because he used to drive a bus; now he was working at the county jail as a deputy sheriff. My mother went by his house and told him, "My son's just seventeen years old, and they got him up there with all them old men. He's got a swollen lip, and he's just a boy. Can you put him with some young men?"

Soon after, I heard a guard come up to the cell and say, "Hooker, roll 'em up." I rolled my stuff up, and I went to another cell block; it felt good to see some young guys. They were glad to see me too.

"We heard what happened down there. You ain't no punk. We heard you put those fists to work."

Still, it felt like a dark cloud was hanging over my head, with my not knowing what was in my future, but the grace of God looked over me. I'm just so thankful for what I went through; it made me who I am today.

Finally, I went to court, and they offered me a plea deal: a five-year suspended sentence if I agreed to go to a drug program. The judge's name was Geraldine Ford, "Ms. Time." She was a woman of little mercy. She said, "Mr. Hooker, this court believes your life is valuable. You're a young man with a future ahead of you. It appears that at some point, you went down the wrong road. We are going to give you a chance to get your life back on track. You're too young to be using drugs and messing up your life. People are dying out there. You can do better. Look at your parents. They love you. Now, do the right thing. Do you want to be helped with your addiction?"

"Yes, your honor," I answered.

The judge continued, "We're sending you to a rehabilitation program called Synanon, a place that will help you curb your addiction and finally get rid of your drug abuse problem. Is the representative from Synanon present in the court at this time?" The representative stood up and raised his hand. "After your release, Mr. Hooker, you will report over to this gentleman's office, and they will instruct you on what to do. I must warn you, Mr. Hooker, if you leave this program within the five years, I will have no other alternative but to send you to state prison for the remaining time. Mr. Hooker, you will be released into the custody of your mother. You are to report to the intake office for Synanon in one week. Do you understand, Mr. Hooker?"

"Yes, I do, your honor."

"Good luck, Mr. Hooker." She said it with a mother's smile, but I read it as "If you don't, I may have to send your Black ass to Jackson Prison quick." She gave me that Big Mama half-closed eye, which was meant as a serious warning about what would happen if I broke my promise. My mother was very happy the judge didn't send her boy to the penitentiary. She looked at me, shook her head, and said, "Boy, if you mess this up, you a fool and out of your mind. You belong in prison."

After my release from custody, we went over to the intake office on Jefferson Boulevard. The information kind of scared me: I had to stay for the entire five years and participate in group-therapy sessions. I would join a very large family of addicts who were supposed to help me. The man at the office said it would be right next to the Pacific Ocean, overlooking the beach. I was thinking, "This sounds really cool; I've never been to a beach." I asked, "Can you smoke in there?" The man said, "Yes, we will provide you with cigarettes." This sounded too good to be true, and I thought about Jackson Prison with no beaches, no girls, and no freedom. I also thought about the Big Mama eye the judge had given me. My mom let me back in her home to get ready. But to be honest, I really didn't want to go. All I wanted right then was a woman and some dope.

The process began. I hugged my sisters Shyvonne, Lavetta, Karen, and Zakiya, as well as my brother Robert, and told them I would miss them. Zakiya encouraged me, "You'll be twenty-one, twenty-two when you get out. You'll still be a young man. Go ahead and get yourself together." I was so sad.

My dad spent the last days with me. We drove around, talked, and bought new socks and underwear. He told me, "We are behind you. The man said that you can't call home for a year, but just know, we are going to be here, and we'll be waiting on you." He also said, "Get off of that stuff. That stuff is going to kill you. You're a young man. When you get out of that place, you can travel with me." He was encouraging me because he knew I didn't want to go.

Both of my parents said, "You'll be alright. Go up there, take care of yourself, come back, and go back to school. Go to college, and get a job. You're better than this, Junior." I just thought about how there wouldn't be any communication with them for a whole year.

But I was still hustling and still using. I was trying to put this Band-Aid over a bullet wound. I got some dope, shot it, and cooked some for the next day. I also had a couple packs of cigarettes; I knew they were going to take them from me when I arrived. You can't bring in any open packages. I remember that day as fresh as anything. There was no TSA back then. I put the dope in some long socks and boarded the plane. When we got to ten thousand feet, the pilot said, "Okay, you're free to move around." I unbuckled my seat belt, went to the bathroom, tied up, shot the dope, and came out. I was so high. There was no turbulence, but I felt like there was. I think the flight attendant knew I was under the influence, so she led me back to my seat, where I just nodded off. When we landed at LAX, I got off, and the people from Synanon were there to pick me up. I could tell right away that they had fake smiles on their faces, so I faked one right back at them.

# 2

# CULT DRUG PROGRAM AND INCARCERATION

# 5

# THE SYNANON CULT

At the time, I didn't know that Synanon began as a drug rehabilitation program but became a religious community and then an evil cult. Founded by Chuck Dederich, the program initiated new members by shaving their heads and forcing them to quit cold turkey. As I learned, their methods were harsh.[1] At first I was taken to a large building and assigned somebody to escort me around. I saw some bald people—men and women walking around, smiling as though all was well—but nothing dawned on me yet, because I was still loaded.

The next day, I met Matthew "Stymie" Beard, my hero from the *Little Rascals/Our Gang*. He stayed at a different facility but was visiting for an open house. It made me happy thinking, "Wow, you too. I'm not the only one that's a dope fiend." It was encouraging in a way: drugs don't discriminate. We shook hands. He told me, "Man, you can do this," and gave me a hug, but at the time, I was still withdrawing.

They assigned me to a place called the "klump." I believe it was an old motel that had been converted into a residence; we were six to a room filled with bunk beds. The next day, they woke me up to get on the bus for breakfast, served in a very large, old dining room. During the first seven days, I was allowed to withdraw without work or responsibilities; I could catch the bus back to the klump, take a shower, or rest. When I returned to the dining room for dinner, if I wanted to, I could stay for a thing called "hoopla," where about sixty or seventy people danced. I watched for a while, but it wasn't for me; I didn't feel good. Every now and then, one of the tribe leaders would ask, "How you doing?"

I'd answer, "I'm doing alright, thank you."

"Well, enjoy your rest time, and get better."

But I was already planning my getaway. I was really sick. I couldn't feed my habit, plus I was homesick and sick of the place. Nobody was talking about dope, which was forbidden, or saying anything negative about the place. Everybody talked about Chuck Dederich as though he were a god.

As soon as the seven days of withdrawal were up, I planned my escape. I couldn't use the phone, and there were no cell phones in 1969. I remembered my dad had said, "Here's a suit to put on so you can look nice just in case you meet a girl." I put on his suit and a tie so that the police wouldn't profile me if they saw me walking down the street. I was used to being stopped and arrested for how I looked. I planned to just walk away, with no idea about which direction to take. I made sure I ate a lot of breakfast that morning so I wouldn't get hungry later on. Everybody then went to work; some had jobs outside of Synanon, and some worked inside. If you'd been there for a year or two and had a business, they let you go to work and pledge your money to them, as though you were a prostitute working for a pimp. While everyone was working, I walked away. The klump wasn't at the beach; it was somewhere in Santa Monica. I walked a long, long way. I did some panhandling, got on a bus, got off, and then continued walking until I saw the Whiskey a Go Go club across Sunset Boulevard, in West Hollywood, and remembered my dad performed there. James Brown was scheduled to perform that weekend. I walked across the street and went to the door, thinking I could ask to use the phone to call my dad, but they were closed, as it was a Monday morning. I got back on the bus and sat until I saw signs showing that I wasn't too far from Beverly Hills; I got off and walked around. Periodically, I saw police cars passing by and became nervous, but they kept going.

I finally got to a phone booth and made a collect call. Nobody was home. I called a half hour later, and my mother picked up and asked, "Where are you, Junior? They let you use the phone? How are you? Are you at that place?"

I answered, "No, but I'm alright."

She said, "You going to jail, Junior. What's wrong with you? Don't you remember what that judge said to you?"

I told her, "I'm not going back to that place. It's really weird, Ma. Everybody is walking around bald-headed. It's strange; it's not for me.

I can kick the habit without all of this." I then asked if my dad was home.

She said, "No, he's out of town. You're just going to have to hang out somewhere until he calls here. Do you remember that lady judge said she was gonna give you five years in prison if you didn't stay there? Boy, you better go back there and try it again."

I answered, "No, I can't go back. I don't even know how to get back there. Plus, I'll be in trouble with them."

I stayed up all night, walking around, sitting in restaurants, and hanging out at bus stops; when I called again, someone said, "Your dad called. Go to the airport." I made it to LAX, went to the counter, and they didn't have my ticket. I sat around in the airport until I finally got my ticket, boarded a plane, and came back to Detroit.

When I arrived, I found out my brother Robert was now taking pills and smoking cigarettes; he had really changed. I was mad at him for taking pills, but at the same time, I felt bad because I probably was the one who'd influenced him to use. I remembered Robert as a chubby guy, and now he was skinny, taking Secos, red devils, and other pills. It broke my heart, but I went back to shooting dope. After living with my sister Zakiya for a while and using dope, she finally had enough and put me out. I went to live with Big Mama on Mack Avenue and Mt. Elliott Street, in her tiny studio apartment where the bathroom was down the hall. Less than three weeks later, I was stopped for being under the influence of drugs and arrested for violating my probation. I went in front of Judge Geraldine Ford again, who looked at me with one eye and said, "I'm going to give you one more chance, Mr. Hooker. The next time, you go to prison. Do you hear me loud and clear?"

I was sent back to Synanon, but not in Los Angeles. This time, it was in Oakland. They picked me up from the airport and took me to a place on the corner of Jefferson and Clay Streets. During the first twelve hours, I had to sit on a bench by the front door because I was deemed a "splittee"—they don't use the word "fugitive." This was a psychological test to see if I would leave or stay. I was allowed to go to the bathroom and eat at a table with only one guy, as I was a bad influence.

After the twelve hours were up, they took me to the barber shop and shaved my head. Then they made me participate in something they called "The Game." They made a circle of thirty or forty people, and someone said, "You, Hooker, get your ass out there in that middle."

I looked around, and someone else said, "You heard what he said. Get your ass in the middle of the floor, boy."

At the same time, everybody was yelling: "Get out there in the middle," "Here's a fool. He left Synanon after they tried to help his stupid ass," and "He don't care. He's a daddy's boy, look. Are you a daddy's boy? Look at me when I'm talking to you, boy."

I tried to defend myself; here were men and women of different races and nationalities talking to me as though I were a punk. I resented it and became very angry.

Someone said, "Shut up, m— f—."

Another White guy said, "Shut up, n—."

Then a Black guy said, "You heard what he said, n—."

I was thinking, "I can't fight back. There's too many of them. This place is holding five years in prison over my head." I was defenseless; I couldn't do anything but listen to the insults.

They cursed me: "I'm gonna make your mama come and kick your ass."

They continued, "Why don't you leave? There's the door. Get your jive ass out of here, you silly little punk." They demeaned me. Tears were rolling from my eyes—I was so mad because I couldn't do anything. They attacked me like that for about forty minutes. Then I heard someone say, "John, there's the door." Everything was quiet. "You can either go out there and die, or you sit there like a man and get that monster out of you. If you want to die, there's the door. You ready to go? Bye. No one will stop you from killing yourself this time."

By now it was dark outside. I had never been to Oakland in my life, and they were saying good-bye. "The Game" then turned to someone else; I sat, wounded. Somebody came up and said, "You'll be alright, man. They do this to everybody. Don't worry about it. I left, too, and they did this to me."

Almost every day, they tried to indoctrinate me into their belief system, to make me believe Dederich was a god and his words were law. Every day in a library, I had to listen to tapes recorded by him, and if not him, then others who quoted his evil doctrines and tried to instill them in me. They gave me assignments and recommendations: "Listen to tape number forty-three, and you'll learn." They quoted Chuck like they were scholars, or like I quote scripture today as a preacher. In the library people were in deep meditation, listening to Dederich. His lessons were psychological. He said you had to look in the mirror and say to yourself, "Self, you are a drug addict, and you will be a drug addict for the rest of your life. But you don't have to succumb to your addiction." It was psychological, but it was manipulation. Dederich believed in hard work, not allowing sex (you had to ask permission "to date"), and making sure no one had too many possessions. He wore sandals, T-shirts, and overalls. People donated used clothes to Synanon; that's what we wore until we were "elevated" to wearing overalls. He also made arbitrary rules, like making sure Synanon had people working twenty-four hours a day. I thought, "The moment I get a chance, I'm getting out of here. But right now, I have to play their game." I knew it was a cult. I thank God that I didn't allow them to brainwash me.

I was not allowed to call home for a year. They would call my family and tell them how great I was doing. Then they would hustle my family out of thousands of dollars. They got my dad for $5,000; I can only imagine how much they got from the rich kids there. I read they'd amassed over $30 million. Men and women gave up their homes and assets—their entire lives.

For the first two months, I cleaned ashtrays and bathrooms while wearing a sign saying, "I am a damn fool." One guy had a sign saying, "I'm a baby's ass." I finally got a maintenance job cleaning floors and carpets on the midnight shift. I had to make sure all the floors were clean and shiny for the next day, when people would come to the place, led by the very saucy talker, John Mahar, who raised millions in donations for Synanon. Slowly, my hair grew back. I stayed there a full year, until I just couldn't take it anymore.

Rumors had been going around that Dederich tried to have somebody murdered.[2] People went missing. I said to myself, "If I rebel, I don't want them to come and get me in the middle of the night, put me in the trunk of a car, dump me in the Pacific Ocean, and then tell my family I got so high I committed suicide. So I played along with the system, smiling, participating in "The Game," and listening to the fake tapes filled with lies and manipulation.

Finally, one day, they told me, "You think you're slick, don't you, Hooker? You're just playing along as though you're part of the establishment, but we're wise to you and to your junkie friends you hang out with. You think we don't see? Get the hell out of here, all of you, and go shoot your dope."

Two weeks before, they had rounded up Eugene Massenburg and his girlfriend, Carmen; George Suttles; and Mario from Puerto Rico and told them to leave. They felt we were a clique—the unprogrammed—so they ran us out one by one (or two by two), with just the clothes on our backs.

When I left, I walked down Clay Street and kept going until I got to the dingy, filthy, red-light-district Monroe Hotel, where prostitutes, pimps, thugs, dope fiends, and dope dealers hung out. I saw Carmen and Eugene coming out of Central's Store on the corner of Jefferson Street. They didn't have any money to get home to New York, so they'd stayed in Oakland. They were hustling: Carmen sold her body, and Gene boosted from department stores. And I did, too, stealing out of cars, stores, and anything else. I stayed in Gene and Carmen's room on the floor, then later transferred to George and his girlfriend's room in the same hotel, where I slept on the chair. One morning, George left the room and said, "I'll be right back, baby." I was under the impression his girl was still asleep, but as soon as the door shut, she looked up at me with a "What's up?" in her eyes. I read what that meant instantly and went over and handled my business; it had been a very long year of not being physically romantic with a woman. Had George entered the room with his key and caught us, he could have killed me; George was six feet, seven inches tall and weighed 275 lbs. When he got back, the girl was gone, and I was standing in the lobby with a guilty look. Suspicious, George kicked me out. Next I stayed with a dope dealer named Kidnap Shorty and his partner; Shorty had done twenty years in San Quentin Prison for kidnapping. He was a short, dark-skinned, evil-looking guy who talked constantly about war stories inside San Quentin. Nobody wants to hear about gang violence.

People who left Synanon in Oakland migrated to the Monroe Hotel; like birds of a feather, they stuck together. We congregated in a little soul-food restaurant next-door to the hotel and upstairs from Central's Store, where there was dope selling and shooting. It was the first time I'd ever seen brown dope. Back East it's all white, but these drugs came from Mexico. As soon as I shot that dope, I hit the ground. *Bam!* I was out, overdosed. Someone called an ambulance; I woke up in Highland Hospital. After they resuscitated me, they kicked me out because I didn't have insurance and was a dope fiend. Life as a dope addict is very difficult; it's no wonder the scriptures say, "The righteous eat to their hearts' content, but the stomach of the wicked goes hungry" (Proverbs 13:25). I wanted peace of mind, to be set free from the gorilla on my back. Here I was again, back out on the street. I decided it was time for me to go home.

# 6

# JACKSON STATE PRISON AND CASSIDY LAKE

I called home and begged my mother and father to send me a ticket; they kept refusing, maybe because they wanted to teach me a lesson or maybe because they were afraid of the five years of prison hanging over my head. After a while, I returned to Detroit and went back to my old ways. Not many days later, I was profiled, picked up for violating my probation, and had to face the same judge. Considering my record of violating probation and the fact that I had been given a second chance, the judge asked, "When are you going to learn you can't go around breaking the law, using drugs, and violating my orders?"

I didn't have any words to respond, because I knew I was dead wrong. The Bible says, "Be sure of this: The wicked will not go unpunished, but those who are righteous will go free" (Proverbs 11:21). My mother was there for the sentencing; the judge asked if there was anything my mother or I wanted to say before she passed the sentence. I shook my head no; my mom asked if I could have one more chance to go back to school. The judge said, "Yes, he can go back to school—in the prison, where he will be going."

It was the day of reckoning for me. I actually got what I deserved: prison. My mom asked the judge if she could have a few minutes to speak with me before they took me away, and the judge granted it. My mother looked at me with that look and said, "Boy, let me tell you something, Junior. You take care of yourself. You hear me? Don't let nothing happen to you. You don't take nothing from nobody."

I said, "Yes, I'll be alright, Ma. Don't worry about me."

I knew what she meant; I was eighteen. And I kept that promise. I was sentenced to two-and-a-half years at Jackson State Prison.

Jackson was built in 1842, and it looked it—old and creepy. It looked like a haunted castle with bars and with pigeons and bats flying around; the convicts looked like the walking dead. We were told to strip naked and there would be no talking; it felt like we were being sold into slavery. They talked to us like we were dogs. They gave us a bar of lye soap and marched us through the shower. While we stood naked, drying off without a towel, they told us to step in a solution to kill whatever germs we might have on our feet. As we stood in the puddle of chemicals, a guy sprayed us in the genital area, then told us to bend over and sprayed us in the anal area. With a loud voice, he said, "Move on." They handed us white jump suits, flip-flops, a smelly chemical blanket, and a fish kit (razor, toothbrush, and comb), then told us to head out in a straight line without talking. They took me to my cell on the ground floor, across from eight block. There was a little bag of something that looked like tree bark to smoke. It was terrible, but I smoked it because I didn't have cigarettes and was desperate.

I was in quarantine for thirty days. When the large door from eight block opened and the lifers and the guys that had gotten twenty to thirty years in general population came out for breakfast, they saw me about a hundred feet away. Some were curious and had a testing look: when they looked at me, I looked back, then looked off, and then looked back again to show them I wasn't scared. Savage inmates look for fear; if they see it, they take advantage. I got along just fine with them; no one bothered me.

I received two visits while I was in Jackson, one from my mother and one from my brother's wife, Lisa. We were good friends; she looked up to me as a big brother. She reported that Robert was doing time in the Detroit House of Correction (DeHoCo); they'd given him six months. I felt bad again. My mother was the worst visitor a person could have; she always reminded me of the chances I'd blown. She said, "Just look at you. Are you satisfied now? You ain't going to be nothing, Junior, if you keep on doing what you been doing. One of these days, if you don't straighten up, you will spend the rest of your life in one of these places."

The prison guards moved me to the fourth tier, next to another youngster, named Walter. He had been to prison before and was a little bit older; he was a cool guy. We made a plan to put our money together to buy cigarettes and to try to get some heroin. There were two Black guys, the White brothers, who had been sentenced to life without parole and worked as nurses' aides. After some negotiations, one of them took our two cartons of cigarettes and came the next day with a package of what looked like heroin. The package was delivered to Walter's cell; he waited until unlock (a scheduled time when cell doors are unlocked to allow for movement) to open the package with me. We tasted it: it was straight-up baking soda. When the next unlock came, Walter and I had our razors, and we caught one of the nurse's aides in the stairwell, walking up the stairs. With our razors out, we said, "Hey man, you think we a bunch of punks? Give us our money back, or your ass is dead." This was a man who was in there for murder, but we just didn't care. We had to show him that even if we were young, he wasn't punking us. Walter and I grabbed him and slammed him against the wall in the stairwell. He said, "I'll get your money back. Somebody must have given me the wrong package."

We thought it was going to be big trouble; these guys were killers. But he brought back the two cartons of cigarettes the very next day. After he returned our cigarettes, we bought some pills from somebody who lived on eight block; the pills just made us laugh hysterically. At about one o'clock in the morning, we were laughing out loud; the guard came by and told us to hold the noise down. People were trying to sleep. We kept laughing, and then we heard the guard say, "I'm going to tell you one more time, hold the noise down, and go to sleep."

That fueled the laughter even more. All of sudden, we heard the guard say into his walkie-talkie, "Open cells forty-four and forty-six." He and another guard walked up and told us to put our hands behind our backs; they handcuffed us and marched us to segregation, or the hole. That was the coldest, darkest place I have ever been. The toilet was a hole in the middle of the floor; you slept—if you could—on the bare floor with a thin blanket. I was thinking, "Oh, my God, what have I done? I'll be good." I slept on the floor with my face toward the bars. That was where they locked people who were gang members or who'd killed guards or other convicts. They only kept us there overnight because we hadn't done anything serious; we were just two goofballs who'd taken some pills.

After quarantine was up, I asked to go to Cassidy Lake, a minimum-security prison.[1] My cousin Junior Mathis had told me to request it because he was already doing time there. Junior and I had grown up together; we were called "them bad two juniors." The family would say, "Don't ever let them get together, 'cause when they get together, honey, they're gonna get in trouble."

Junior, Robert, and I would go fishing together with my mother's brothers, Uncle Frank Eddie and Junior's father, Uncle Nig. Uncle Nig had gotten his nickname—his real name was William—when they were on a plantation in Arkansas. Big Mama told me the White folks gave him that name: Nig—you know what the rest of it is. But Nig was his name to the whole family, including his own mother, all except for his wife, Aunt Lois. She called him William. Uncle Frank Eddie and Uncle Nig would call my mother and ask if Robert and I wanted to go fishing with them. Sometimes we'd go fishing through the tunnel into Windsor, Canada. They knew a very good spot in the marshes.

Whenever Junior and I got into a fight, I would beat him up and win. He telegraphed his punches; he would pull way back, like he was trying to throw a curveball at a baseball game. I'd punch, grab, and put him in a headlock and wrestle him to the ground, then he'd cry. He would run and try to grab something, but I'd be gone. Junior and I also got into trouble together: we got high, stole, and chased girls in the neighborhood. We went to the liquor store connected to the pharmacy where we used to buy Robitussin cough syrup. At fifteen we were drinking and breaking into cars. If we got fifty dollars, it was big money. The Robitussin led to marijuana and drinking that turned into snorting and shooting heroin.

Many weekends Robert and I would spend the night at Uncle Nig and Aunt Lois's house. They had a basement where they gambled and where Junior, Robert, and I all would sleep in the same rollaway bed. We would joke and laugh all night. One time, after Junior was hooked on dope, he went downstairs to where his big sister, Dolores; his mother, Aunt Lois; Big Mama and her boyfriend Big Jesse; and Uncle Frank Eddie's girlfriend Frieda were all playing poker, and he pulled out a rifle. I wasn't there, but Dolores told me he said, "Don't nobody move. Give me all the money. Empty your purses, and put your wallets on the table."

Dolores was a big girl, about six feet, four inches tall and around 200 lbs. She said, "I told that fool, 'You ain't going to do nothing. Ain't nobody giving you a dime, boy. Put that damn gun down now, Junior.'"

She walked up, grabbed the rifle, wrestled him to the floor, and beat him up. He started crying and ran out the door.

Big Mama corroborated the story: "Do you know what that boy did? He came down there with a gun and told us, 'Don't nobody move.' And I said, 'Junior, if you don't put that gun down, I'm going to get up here and take my shoe and beat the mess out of you!' It's a good thing Dolores got him, 'cause I was going to whup his ass too." They didn't call the police; if they had, his armed robbery attempt would have given him ten to fifteen years in the pen in Michigan. But he made enemies that night; no one ever trusted him again.

Growing up, Junior and I weren't always together, but every now and then, we'd run into each other and shoot dope or hit a lick together. Finally, Junior went to prison for burglary. He got two-and-a-half years for breaking and entering. He was in before me; we were allowed to write each other letters from prison, and our family would pass along messages. He told me to request Cassidy Lake, where he was. And if I didn't get Cassidy Lake, I figured they would send me to the "gladiator school," Ionia, the do-or-die penitentiary, where you either walk out alive or are carried out on a stretcher.

I didn't know it at the time, but there's a point system based on your record. With violence, sex crimes, and other serious offenses, you get a high score and are sent to Ionia or Marquette. Because it was my first offense and my points were very low, I was sent to Cassidy Lake. After being in the dirty, evil Jackson Prison, I felt like Cassidy Lake was Disneyland. Everybody was walking around free: there were no fences, guards wore street clothes, and everybody was smoking cigarettes. Junior had me set up; he'd told everybody his cousin was coming. I was put in the same cabin with Junior, and we were bunkies. He'd saved the top bunk for me. He'd even gotten me a job in the kitchen with the head-cook supervisor, Bull, an ex-professional cook from the streets, who taught me how to cook. Junior bused tables and cleaned up. He introduced me to everybody. They called him Bear, as he was this big round guy. There were no fences at Cassidy Lake. You could run off if you wanted to. The guards working in the front office and walking the compound were there just to make a show of it.

A guy named Bay Bay Jones had been in Ionia a while and was a pretty good boxer; he seemed to me the bully of the camp. One day he and Junior got into a confrontation. One thing about prison is you have to go down with your kinfolk or your homies, even if they're dead wrong. I didn't know if Junior was right or wrong, I just saw him walking the grounds with this look. I asked, "What's wrong with you?"

Holding a long, sharp pencil in his hand, he said, "Bay Bay Jones's talking to me like I'm a punk."

Bay Bay came up and asked, "What you want to do, Bear?"

I was standing with Junior, thinking, "There's going to be an attempted murder—Junior's going to stab him in the face. Then I'm gonna have to grab Bay Bay, hold him, and land a few blows. I've got to back my cousin up." I knew Bay Bay expected me to. But it simmered out. Even though he knew he was good with his fists, Jones could see the rage in Junior's face, and I was not smiling. He couldn't whup both of us. After that no one spoke, but everything began to relax.

One weekend, Bull, the cook supervisor, went on vacation, and our friend who was the head cook left the kitchen window open at our request. The head cook inmate, Mims; Junior; Luther Rutherford; and I all went in. It was Mims's first time being in prison, and he could really cook. Bull had taught him everything. We had wine brewing in a bucket for about four days. We stole yeast from the bakery, as well as fruit, juices, and rice, and mixed them together; this started to bubble and turned into wine. We got drunk every week off the pruno. We went into the butcher's refrigerator and cooked up pounds of chicken in the deep-fry kettle. When the chicken was done, we cleaned up and took the chicken up to our barracks on a hill. We had a big spread, like a picnic party. People came from every cabin with marijuana, drugs, and hashish to have with some chicken and wine. We drank, smoked, laughed, ate, and danced while we listened to music, and we had a good time. Nobody told, and nobody ever got caught. Imagine a party in the penitentiary: getting high on dope and eating the state's fried chicken.

After about six months, Junior was released. I was sad to see him go; he was the only one I'd hung out with. But before I got out, I heard Junior Mathis was back, doing his thing: shooting dope and robbing, plus the parole officer was looking for him. When I was released three or four months later, Junior came over to our house to welcome me home, but it was really to get high with me. I went right back to it too: we got in his car and went straight to the dope house. It came to pass, just like our parents told us: "Once a junkie, always a junkie." Junior violated parole and was arrested. After six months of good behavior, he was allowed to go to the halfway house. While he was supposed to be out on a pass to search for employment, he pulled an armed robbery and got nine years in Macomb Correctional Facility—he had only been in the halfway house for two weeks. Junior was told that the next time he would be given life in prison as a habitual criminal. It went in one ear and out the other.

# 7

# CALIFORNIA
## CRIMES, HEISTS, AND
## THE CON GAME

Shortly after I got out of prison in 1971, my dad called and said, "If you don't get out of Detroit, you going to get killed or end up right back in prison. You need to get out of the ghetto and come to California." He had moved to San Francisco while I was in prison; while I was still on parole, my dad sent for me. I was the first one in the family to move out to California with him. At first I stayed with him as his roommate; we were at the Chronicle Hotel on Mission Street in a one-bedroom apartment with a pullout couch. He was playing at the Keystone Korner, owned by Freddie Herrera, in North Beach. Herrera also had a Keystone club in Palo Alto. People started booking my dad all over Northern California: Berkeley, San Francisco, Palo Alto, and Santa Cruz. They all fell in love with John Lee Hooker.

Next, we moved to the Jackson Apartments in Oakland, near downtown and close to beautiful Lake Merritt. My dad and I were roommates again, but this time, it was a two-bedroom apartment. One day he heard me singing in the bathroom. When I came out, he said, "Boy, b-b- b-b- but you can sing, boy," and he encouraged me to run with my talent, saying he'd help in any way he could—but I had to leave dope alone. The first time he brought me onstage, I was so nervous that I was out of key and didn't know how to come in. I sang "Too Many Drivers" by Lowell Fulsom. My voice was cool, but I was scared. At the end of the song, when nobody clapped, my dad said, "Give him a round of applause," and then loud clapping began.

After I got paid for singing at different gigs, my dad would say, "Bye." That meant to hurry up and get out of there; he had a lady coming by. Lex Silva, his bass player, would drive me down to cop some dope at the same Monroe Hotel I'd discovered after Synanon. Lex shot dope, too, and would later die of a heroin overdose.

At some point, I briefly went back to Detroit while my dad was touring in Europe. A few months after I got off parole, my dad sent for me again—this time, for good. My dad's driver Clint picked me up at the airport. By now my dad was really established. He'd bought a three-story, four-bedroom house with three bathrooms on Buena Ventura Avenue in the Oakland Hills. From the balcony you could see all over the Bay Area. It was beautiful. My dad liked to brag to his kids but not to anybody else. When I stepped inside the door, my dad said, "Welcome to my mansion, boy. This ain't n-n-n-n-no Detroit. You ain't in the ghetto no mo'. You better straighten up up here, boy, or they'll put you away for good." I had the whole bottom floor to myself: a room with a shower, a bar, and a sliding door. I thought, "My own apartment: girls, girls, get high, and get high."

Huey Newton hired my dad to play a concert for the Black Panther Party at the Oakland Auditorium, where they gave away ten thousand bags of groceries. At the time, Newton was campaigning to be mayor of Oakland, and the Panthers were boycotting Safeway supermarkets in solidarity with the United Farm Workers. I was the featured singer; as I was leaving, I met a beautiful sister named Ayesha, who had a significant impact on my life. She was the prettiest Black girl I had ever seen, with her ebony skin and beautiful wavy hair tied in a ponytail. We hit it off and exchanged numbers. The next day, she called and told me she had just left downtown San Francisco and was headed to Oakland, to the bus stop at the post office near Lake Merritt. I drove down, picked her up, brought her back to my home, and introduced her to my dad. He commented on how pretty she was right in front of her: "Boy, you got a pretty one. Keep her, Junior, and treat her right." Then he asked her, "Can you cook?" and laughed out loud.

We fell in love superficially. Before we left for a tour the following month, I asked my dad if I could take her with us. My dad thought she was nice and didn't seem like trouble, so he agreed. She went with us on tour as far as Seattle, then we got into an argument when I learned she was trying to get pregnant. Before we had sex the first time, she told me she had something inside of her to prevent her from getting pregnant, an old-school sponge. After we finished making love, she told me she had removed it and was trying to have a child. I was angry; I felt she should have talked to me about it. She was sent home on a bus. Ayesha later called and told me she was pregnant. At the time, I was on drugs and in and out of prison, then in a drug program. When her sister called my dad's house to say they were looking for me because Ayesha had given birth to my son, someone gave her the number of the drug program, and she explained the situation to the director. It was bittersweet to me because of the position I was in: I was allowed to visit San Francisco General Hospital to see them—with an escort. The hospital staff took me to Ayesha's room and her face was all broken out; that's what happens to drug addicts when they're withdrawing. I told her I was in a drug program, trying to get better, and said I hoped she got better too. I didn't have any romantic feelings for her; our relationship felt hopeless. It was just bad for both of us.

Ayesha named my son Johnny. He was a beautiful child, who looked just like his mama; he was born with cocaine in his system and had to be treated with medication. He was really small, crying, and shaking. I could see he was suffering with withdrawals. I felt like a loser, which I was. I couldn't look at either of them anymore and left with my escort.

Her life went on; my life spiraled down. Many years later, while I was in San Jose County Jail for a grand theft arrest, she wrote me a letter and told me my son was doing fine. She asked me to leave them alone. She was engaged to a doctor who really cared about her. I told her I wanted visitation for my son but soon got a letter from a civil judge telling me I would not be getting custody or visitation. It said if I continued to press the matter, they would file an injunction against me and I would have to pay thousands of dollars in child support. I got the message and left them alone.

Fast forward to many years later, I heard through the grapevine that Ayesha had hooked up with Johnny "Guitar" Watson and moved to Los Angeles. He wrote a song, "I Want to Ta-Ta You Baby," about her. Ayesha was in communication with my sister Diane throughout our estrangement. When my dad received a star on the Hollywood Walk of Fame, Ayesha came and handed Diane a newspaper clipping, which she brought back and showed me. It was an obituary. My son had grown up, and at nineteen, he was murdered in Los Angeles. He'd become a Crip gang member. Ayesha sent me pictures of him doing all the gang signs.

What a wasted life—my heart was broken. Ayesha and I became friends for the remainder of her life.

Years later, Ayesha contacted me via Facebook Messenger and told me she was in hospice care. She never disclosed the diagnosis, but I think it was probably cancer; she chose to die at home. We exchanged Facebook messages and talked over the phone. By that time ministry had become my life. I thought the right thing to do was to adhere to the word of God: Jesus said about visiting the sick, "Truly I tell you, whatever you did for one of the least of these brothers and sisters of mine, you did for me" (Matthew 25:40). My way of representing the kingdom of God was to go and pay my last respects; I flew down to Los Angeles, rented a car, and drove to her apartment. She sat on the couch in her housecoat and told me she was optimistic about beating her death sentence; she tried indirectly to convince me to give her $40,000 for an operation to help her live longer, but I didn't have that kind of money. We talked and she was happy to see me. I gave her $200 to help her out, but I could see there was disappointment in her face when she opened the envelope with a card inside: she was looking for the $40,000. I asked to pray for her, and she reluctantly agreed. As I prayed, she gave me one of those looks like, "Please hurry up and say amen." My visit was brief; I think she felt let down.

A week or two after that, I was scheduled to have a gospel concert at our church in Sacramento, Progressive COGIC. Ayesha had decided that if she was going to die, she was going to enjoy her last days. I got a message that she was going to come up with another ex-girlfriend of Johnny "Guitar" Watson's. My sisters Shyvonne, Lavetta, and Karen were also there. While I had the microphone, I acknowledged Ayesha and told the audience what she had said about enjoying her last days on earth. Before Ayesha left with her friend, I gave her a check for $150 for gas and a hotel. I thanked her for coming up; that was the last time I saw her.

During the 1970s my brother Robert and I always hustled together. One time I snatched all the dope from a dealer at the Monroe Hotel. He was not a "reputable" dealer; this was a new booty who was hustling and violating turf rules. Dealers were being robbed because the Robinson Crew—Fox, Big Herman, and their little brother Cornell—weren't always around. This was a great opportunity for me; I went in and asked for two sacks. When the new dealer pulled out all the dope in a plastic

Ziploc bag, I faked like I had a gun in my pants and said, "Don't move, fool." I ran out the door and jumped in the van. I said to my brother, "Step on it. Let's go." People were running behind me.

Because Robert used to race illegally in Detroit, betting money against other drivers, when he hit it, he really hit it! It was truly crazy; my name and my dad's name were painted all over the van for promotion. Who would rob the dope man with "John Lee Hooker featuring John Lee Hooker Jr." painted on the side of the van? Drug addicts do dumb stuff. We headed east to the Park Street Bridge, toward Alameda. That wasn't really our destination, but that's where we went. Robert was flying way above the speed limit. He hit a right-hand turn down Twenty-Ninth Avenue, toward the drawbridge as it was coming up. I said, "Step on it," and Robert jumped the drawbridge. We got away from the guys chasing us. When we pulled in somewhere and parked, both of us breathing heavily, I showed him all the dope. He said, "You a damn fool, Junior. You crazy. You almost got us killed."

I said, "Yeah, but we gonna die feeling good." He laughed and shook his head as we drove home to east Oakland and headed straight for my living quarters, downstairs. Three weeks later, we went back to the Monroe Hotel, and the dealer wasn't there. We never saw him again.

The Monroe Hotel was full of every kind of human being: pimps, prostitutes, cutthroats, killers, dealers—you name it, they all hung out there. I learned how to play the con game there from a guy named Al. He showed me the "Jamaican bomb." For this con game, you say you're from Jamaica and talk like someone from the island. Everything is "mon," said with a Jamaican accent. We would make a "mish": a fake bankroll that was the size of dollar bills and made of cut-up newspapers. It had $2 bills on the top and bottom and was tied together in a $25,000; $50,000; or $75,000 money wrap from a bank.

Al would go up to someone and say, "Can you help me find dis place?" and show them a property tag with a fictitious hotel address on it. He continued, "Look, I'm gonna tell you one time, if you can help me find dis place, I cannot make you rich, but I help you with a gift." Then he would flash the fake bank roll. People would agree to help because they had larceny and greed in their hearts. An honest person would have said, "This is a job for the police." If the mark suggested we go to the police, Al would say, "I no trust them because them did something to my mother back in Jamaica."

CHAPTER 7

The con went as follows: Al has inherited a large sum of money. But he can't take the money back to Jamaica; people there are looking for him because his family owes the government money. He wants someone to donate the money because it's useless to him, but he wants someone who is worthy and not greedy. He is looking for someone he can trust to hold the money while he goes back to Jamaica.

Once he had a mark, Al would pull on his collar to signal to me, the "cap man," to walk alongside them. Al would say, "Maybe we can find somebody to tell us if they know dis place I'm looking for." If the mark said, "Let's ask this man," that was the best, but if he didn't, Al would stop me. I'd look at the address and say, "Let me see, I've heard of this place." Then Al would pull out the fake bankroll and offer us both a gift. I'd say to the mark, "Why you let him flash all that money?" I would tell the "Jamaican" to put the money away before he was robbed or killed. The mark would usually agree about the danger of flashing all that money.

There were two ways to get the mark: the "trust" and the "switch." If we were both really sick and needed dope right away, we would "trust" it off. Al would say he needed to go back to Jamaica and wait until his brother could get a passport and visa to return with him to live in the United States. The mark had to keep the money until they returned in thirty days because Al didn't trust "the white mon's bank." Al said he'd give the mark and me each $40,000 and even offered to pay right then.

I would say, "You don't have to pay us now, only when we fulfill our promise to you. But you know what? You can't trust everybody. If you're going to let somebody hold all that money, sir, you got to be able to trust them. They have to be a law-abiding citizen with a job. Ain't that right, Mark?"

The mark would agree. Then I'd pull out my wallet—likely without anything to show—but we'd stand on the blind side of the mark so he couldn't see inside as Al pretended to check my ID and count the money. Al would say, "Oh yes, you have hundred-dollar bills in jo wallet."

I would say, "Please don't disclose what I have, sir. It's very dangerous out here these days." Then I'd say, "He can show you that he can be trusted as well. Show him, sir." Then the mark showed his ID and all his money. To test the mark to make sure Al could trust him with the money while he "returned" to Jamaica, he asked the mark to walk around the block with my money. I would say, "Take this money, put it in your back pocket, and walk around that corner." The Jamaican would walk around the block with the mark to make sure he didn't run away. When they'd come back, Al would say, "Him no act like the long-finger robber man. I can trust. Okay, I pay for you right now." Then he'd say, "But hold it just a one minute. I see that you trust him, but how do I know if him trust you?"

So, I say, "Mark, gimme that money you got."

The mark would go in his pocket and give up his wallet. Sometimes he'd have $700 or $800. I would say, "Mark, which way did y'all go?"

He'd reply, "We just went around the corner."

I'd say, "Okay, I'll be right back."

The "Jamaican" then would ask the mark if he could go along with me like he'd done with him. He'd reply, "Sure, I trust you." We'd walk, and as soon as we'd hit the corner, we were gone. That was called the "trust," which got us a quick and sometimes big, other times small, amount of money.

The way to get more money was the "switch," or "double drag." Texas Bill, Short Coat, and Mellow Mel were guys who taught me how to play the game. Someone would pretend to be from South Africa and carry a letter vouching for them; it looked authentic with the South African flag and a fake signature from Bishop Desmond Tutu. The story went that the person had received a $200,000 settlement from Chevron in San Diego because his brother was killed while working on a job. He couldn't take the first $100,000 of the money back to South Africa, because the government would think that he was in the African National Congress (ANC) and intending to use it to buy weapons. He needed a reliable person to hold it and eventually distribute the money to a worthy charity. From there it was the same as the "trust": you had to make sure that the mark was "reliable" and "trustworthy." We prepared the mish: four stacks of money with $25,000 bands around fake bills. Someone played the South African and flashed the mish while I played the cap man. In this con we first "dragged" the mark to the bank to demonstrate we were trustworthy, and then he'd withdraw a few thousand dollars to show he could be trusted. I carried a "knot"—a newspaper made to look like a bankroll with half of a bandana wrapped around it—in my sweater, which was to be switched with the real money. After the mark withdrew the money from the bank, the South African would say he could see that he could trust the mark. He then gave them all his money—the mish—to hold. After the mark put the money away, the South African would say, "Hold it just one minute. Why you put my money there? I afraid the long-finger robber man can come along and take it away, and me have nottin' when me come back."

I'd ask him, "What do you suggest?"

The South African would say, "Give it to me. Let me show you." He'd pull out the other half of the bandana that the knot was wrapped in and tie up the real money in a tight knot. Then he'd say, "You put it next to the heart to keep the evil spirits away," which he'd demonstrate by putting the money under his arm. He'd then quickly drop the real money from his armpit, switch it for the fake money, and hand it back to the mark, saying, "Do it lika dis. This way I know you'll fight like Muhammad Ali if somebody tries to take the money."

We'd walk out to the car, and I'd tell the mark to open the trunk. After the mark put the money in, I'd say, "Please do the right thing."

The mark usually said, "I will."

And I'd say, "I'll see you in two hours, after I take him to a hotel for the night."

We'd get in the car, give each other high fives, split the money, and drive to west Oakland to get some dope.

While I was working the con with Al, I witnessed my first murder. I was coming out of his room at the Monroe Hotel, high as a kite. As I was walking down the hall, I saw André kick Dirty Bob's door in. I took a few steps and could see Dirty Bob in the corner, begging for his life. I kept walking, and next thing I heard was *pow, pow, pow*! As I headed down the stairs, André skipped stairs and ran past me, out the door. We were only half a mile from the Oakland Police Department, so an ambulance got there right away. I saw them bring Bob down on a stretcher, with his guts hanging out. He said, "Bam Bam, help me." But there was nothing I could do. They called him Dirty Bob because he would rob you and run off with your dope. He'd done something to the wrong person. Dirty Bob died before he could get to the hospital, but he was able to tell the police who'd shot him before he died. The police came back and offered a couple of bags of heroin to people to give up names; they had informants. They never came to me, but they must have gotten somebody because André got fifteen years to life.

The Monroe Hotel was one of the coldest and most dilapidated places in Oakland. Overdose was my nickname. People knew I had money because I was a con player. One time, when I fell out in Big

Ricky's room, he dragged me to the common bathroom down the hall and shut the door. I woke up in this funky, nasty bathroom with my pants' pockets turned out. He must have gotten at least $500 out of my pocket; I had just taken a mark. Now I was the mark out of all of my money.

**3**

# MUSIC, PRISONS, AND CON GAMES

# 8

# CANADIAN TOUR AND PRISON

During the early 1970s, I performed with my dad all over the United States and Canada at everything from small venues to big festivals. For a twenty-seven-day tour of Canada, we started in Seattle (where Ayesha and I argued). We continued our tour to Toronto, Winnipeg, Kamloops, Calgary, Saskatoon, Edmonton, Montreal, Victoria, and Regina. Cliff Swank, my dad's road manager, was also the van driver. The band members were Ken Swank, who was on drums, Gino Skaggs on bass, Luther Tucker on guitar, and Robert Hooker on keyboard; they are all deceased now. It was so beautiful but bittersweet, as I was hooked on dope; all I thought about was how and where to get drugs. Sometimes I cried in my room; I wasn't enjoying myself. The others were laughing like normal people while I was scheming about how to cop.

Every show in every city sold out. I opened the show as the featured attraction; I sang two or three songs to pump up the crowd and then introduced "the king of the boogie, my father and your father of the blues, the Boogie Man himself, Mr. John Lee Hooker." The crowd went wild, screaming, shouting, and stomping their feet, and he would just stand there for about thirty seconds, then sit down and yell, "Are you ready?"

"Yeahhhhh," the crowd would answer back.

Then he would say, "Another round of applause for John Lee Hooker Jr." When he'd finish his last song, he'd play a boogie, stand up, and say, "Are you ready to boogie?" After about three minutes of bringing the crowd to their feet with wild screams, he'd motion for me to come out and join him; the crowd would go berserk. After we'd traded verses back and forth, he'd wave his hand and take a bow. I would end the show with "Ladies and Gentlemen, please give a round of applause to Mr. John Lee Hooker!"

There were interviews, cameras, and women at every city, every stop, every break: one-night stands, sex, drugs, and alcohol. My dad didn't use any drugs or weed or smoke cigarettes, only an occasional beer, but I saw band members cheat on their wives and girlfriends. Women traveled to the next city to be able to join whichever band member they'd been with the night before, only to be told good-bye; one-night stands were standard procedure on the road. My dad was a straight player. He had a pretty woman every night. When I opened for B. B. King many years later, he called me into his dressing room and said, "I ain't seen you in a long time, young man. You look just like your daddy. Me and your dad and Ray Charles, we were all dirty old men." He was smiling and shaking his head as he said it. I should note that, at that time in Canada, my dad wasn't married, and neither was I. I followed his lead. My dad would say, "Look at them girls looking at you, boy. Look at that one over there," and he'd point one out. Like father, like son.

I never once saw my brother Robert with another lady, but I had my suspicions; he was a smooth operator and did everything under the radar. I didn't look his way before or after the gigs—it was "Hear no evil, see no evil" for me—but I saw pretty women taking a good look at him. I'm going to leave that alone. If he'd done it, he was slicker than a worm on a rainy day.

I preyed relentlessly on the opening acts: going into their dressing rooms, searching their belongings, and sometimes finding huge amounts of money, drugs, and jewelry. They had no clue who'd ripped them off; however, my dad and the band had their suspicions. When someone asked, "Did you see anyone go in or come out of our dressing room?" I was the cat with the canary's feathers around my mouth. I wasn't able to cop heroin in every city; alcohol, free cocaine, and pills were my substitutes until I'd hit the jackpot and pass out in a hotel room. My dad also tried to help me with my sickness, giving me Valium if I couldn't sleep because of withdrawals.

We got to Vancouver, the last city on the tour. I had run out of dope and was getting sick; I had to feed the gorilla on my back the entire tour. During a show I met people and asked where I could get some weed—you'd never ask about heroin or cocaine. One guy told me to go to the Gastown Saloon. When I got there, I asked someone, "Where can I get some weed?"

He said, "Right in here."

I asked, "What else they got?"

"Whatever you want."

Before anyone would sell me some dope, he said, "How do I know you aren't the police?" I pulled up my sleeve and showed him my tracks; he nodded his head. A guy at the Gastown Saloon sold me some China White. When I got back to the hotel, I also had some Valium with me. Anybody will tell you, "Don't mix pills when you're shooting heroin—especially not Valium—or you're going to OD and might not wake up again." But I was a greedy dope fiend; I took the Valium and dope together to enhance my high. *Boom!* I fell on the floor, completely out.

After coming to I took a shower and got ready for the show. Before I went out, I thought I needed more drugs. I went to the opening act's dressing room and stole about $700; they never reported it. Then I went out on stage, danced around, sang two songs, and introduced my dad: "Ladies and gentlemen, are you ready for the blues? Help me bring on, with a round of applause, his majesty, the king of the blues himself, my father and the king of the boogie, John Lee Hooker." He walked out and looked at me—he was mad because I'd taken too long; he could tell I was high. The drugs had made me feel like it was my show. After I left the stage, I called a taxi and headed back to the Gastown Saloon. I found the guy, got some heroin, went back to my room, and got high.

I went back to the Gastown Saloon several times. One time I was broke and about to be sick, so I tried to rob the dealer. You couldn't sell dope in the saloon, so I maneuvered him out to the parking lot. I thought I could bluff him because I had an acrylic dagger. I grabbed his dope and pulled the knife: "Don't move, punk." As I was heading to the vehicle with drugs in my hand, the guy fought back hard and would not give up. After ten minutes of wrestling and boxing, the struggle was over; exhausted, I gave him his dope back. He let me keep one little pill. I'd never had anybody fight me like that; I must admit that White boy whupped me. He fought me for those drugs as though he were supporting seven kids, taking care of his mother and father and the cat and the dog, and had rent to pay . . . no one was taking his money on that day.

We were in Vancouver for a few days, and soon I was broke again. This time I took the tour van with my father's and my name painted on it. I took the drums, bass, and amplifiers, and I pawned everything—even my father's guitar. I was a lowdown dog with no conscience, the epitome of evil. With the money from the pawn shop, I drove to Gastown, bought some more dope, and got loaded. I was so high that I passed out behind the wheel and wrecked the van. It's only by the grace of God I didn't die. The van was torn up. When I woke up, I saw a guy speaking French, sticking his feet in and out of the toilet, and flushing it over and over. I thought I'd woken up in hell but soon realized I was in jail. After seeing a judge, I was released on my own recognizance; I didn't have a record in Canada, and at the time, they had no idea I had a police record in the United States.

I was supposed to go back to court the next day, but I didn't. I got so loaded in the hotel room that I nodded out at the desk with dope and the cooker in front of me. I heard a knock on the door, and somebody said, "Open up in the name of the Royal Canadian Mounted Police." They kicked the door in and took me to jail for driving under the influence and failure to appear. My dad came to see me and said, "Boy, you got my name all over the newspaper and ringing on the radio too. I'm embarrassed. Where's the pawn ticket for the instruments? I should let you rot here. Don't you ever ask to go do a tour with me. I'm going to get you a lawyer. And don't, don't, don't, don't call me no more. You hear me?"

After getting the van repaired, my dad and the band went back to California. The lawyer got me ninety days in Oakalla Prison Farm, or the Lower Mainland Regional Correctional Centre. The judge said, "Mr. Hooker, I can see you have no respect for the Canadian government; for that we're giving you ninety days. Once your sentence is over, you have forty-eight hours to leave this country. If you do not, we will arrest you again, and you will be subject to a greater sentence."

When I arrived at the prison, the news was blaring on the radio, "The son of John Lee Hooker was arrested and sentenced to ninety days." I could hear them on the tiers, saying, "He's right down there. There he goes." I was this infamous guy, recognized all over the prison for doing something only a dope fiend would do: going to another country and getting arrested. I got a job working near the front office in receiving and release. If someone came in with any dope, I was the guy who could get it in; they never strip searched the workers. Sometimes I got a simple pat down, and sometimes they would just say, "Go on." The inmates paid me off with some of the dope. An American like me couldn't come in and take over the drug trade, or something might happen, so I made sure to pass out dope to some of the big shots just to keep the peace. Though I was greedy, I wasn't that dumb.

One day there was an announcement, "Attention on the yard. John Lee Hooker Jr., you have a visit." I was fifty days into my sentence, and my dad and everyone had gone; I wondered who it could be. I went to the visiting hall and walked from window to window to see if anyone would call to me. This skinny lady stood up and waved me over. Her name was Diane. She said, "I met your bass player, Gino Skaggs, at the gig. I heard you were locked up in here, and I thought I'd come down and see if you needed anything."

I said, "Wow, thank you for asking. I can use a few dollars."

She left me fifty dollars on my books and was up there every week to visit me, sometimes twice a week. Finally, she told me, "When you get out in four weeks, I'll be here to pick you up. You're a cool guy, John. When you get out, I got something for you."

The way she said it, I knew it had to be sex and maybe a little something else—I didn't know. Remember, once released, I had forty-eight hours to get out of Canada. My dad had left me a plane ticket on my books. The day I was released, she picked me up in a van. She jumped out and gave me a kiss, like I was her boyfriend, then she took me on a route. I learned this woman was a big-time dope dealer in Vancouver. She got out of the van and told me to wait there; out of the sideview mirror, I could see her coming back, carrying a large box. I learned it was hashish. I got out to help, and she said, "I got it."

She made another stop. This time she got several pounds of marijuana. When we got to her place, people were hanging out there, as though they were expecting me. She told me to sit down, turned on the radio, and said, "I have a surprise for you." The announcer came on and said, "We want to dedicate this next song to John Lee Hooker Jr. Welcome home, Junior." I was thinking, "This girl's got big-time juice."

Diane's girlfriend walked over to me and handed me a folded-up pack of paper shaped like a heart. I opened it, and there was at least a half ounce of cocaine inside. I realized most of the people there were dealers. She took me to a nightclub, and here was another surprise: someone announced, "We'd like to invite Mr. John Lee Hooker Jr. up to the stage. Let's give him a round of applause." I got up, and the band played a slow blues. I sang "Sweet Sixteen" by B. B. King, and everyone went bananas. We returned to her place and had sex. I was supposed to leave within forty-eight hours, and it had already been seventy-two. That turned into a week. Luckily, she didn't deal heroin, or I would have been dead. Finally, I knew it was time for me to go before I got caught. I could hear my dad's voice: "Don't call me." But the plane ticket he'd left for me had expired. I had to call my dad to get another ticket. Diane took me to the airport, crying like we'd known each other for fifty years. I gave her a hug and a kiss and headed home. That's when the border services agents told me, "Don't ever come back to Canada, Mr. Hooker."

I did come back sometime in the 2000s, to tour with my band. Someone cleared me to come across the border; I was very surprised and excited to go back. The next time we tried to go to Canada, they charged us $1,500. The third time we tried, someone new was in charge. He said, "I don't know how you got in here in the first place," and I was denied entrance and told never to come back.

When I got back to Oakland, I went back to shooting dope and playing the con game. At some point I was picked up for a parole violation while under the influence and sent to a drug program, which is where I was when Ayesha gave birth to Johnny. In fact, my escort and I had been told to go right back to the program after we'd visited the hospital, but we went to my dad's house. I needed money to buy toiletries, underwear, and other things. I took the money and asked the escort, "How you feel?" My eye contact said, "You ready?" We left my dad's house, went to the Monroe Hotel or West Oakland, got some dope, and shot it. The stress of seeing Ayesha in that condition and the baby suffering from withdrawals had devastated me. Out came the Band-Aid again—to get it off my mind. We were so high when we got back to the program that they told us to get out.

# 9

# MARIE'S OVERDOSE
# AND SANTA RITA JAIL

My dad's house on Buena Ventura Avenue was a thoroughfare for celebrities, fans, and beautiful women from all over the world; they came from France, England, Japan, Australia, and throughout the United States to hang out with and meet the Boogie Man. I met this beautiful girl named Marie; she came out with a lady named Vicky to the Catalyst in Santa Cruz to see us play. My dad had a brief encounter with Vicky, who then brought her girlfriend Marie back to the house in Oakland one day. Marie and I got really friendly and became boyfriend and girlfriend; we were both wild and liked to party and get high. Marie was a real sweetheart—100 percent hippie, always laughing and smiling. She knew I was a slickster and had been in prison. She told me she knew a place we could rip off to get drugs and money. We jumped in the car and drove to a house; I parked while Marie went to the door. After she knocked and there was no answer, she went around to the back, stayed inside for about fifteen minutes, and came out with a shopping bag filled with jars of pills, packages of weed, and lots of money. We both laughed with excitement, split the scene of the crime, and headed to the Monroe Hotel to get some heroin. She let it be known that she didn't like me shooting dope; she was a pot smoker, took pills, and drank alcohol. So after the robbery, she smoked and drank while I shot.

After six months together, I came home one day and went downstairs. I didn't see Marie in the bedroom, but I heard water running in the bathroom and figured she was taking a shower. I shot my dope; after I finished, I called her name, but she didn't answer. I called again and knocked on the door; again, no answer. I picked the lock with an old expired credit card, and when I opened the door, Marie was lying in the corner with a syringe in her arm and gelatin caps around her, with her eyes open and tints of blue on the skin of her face. I recognized the bluish-red gelatin pills as the ones she had stolen; Marie had shot too much, and her heart had stopped pumping. The scriptures say, "They will eat the fruit of their ways and be filled with the fruit of their schemes" (Proverbs 1:31). She died from the same dope she'd stolen. I quickly ran upstairs and told my dad that Marie was dead of an overdose and dialed 911. He knew I wasn't responsible; he came down and saw the body himself. He said, "Don't touch her, Junior. Wait until the ambulance gets here." He even called her name: "Marie!" My dad held me in his arms and patted me on my back as I cried like a baby. She was my first real love. I'd had girlfriends in Oakland, Santa Cruz, Sacramento, and Palo Alto, but Marie had been my partner in crime. The paramedics arrived with the police and asked questions. Then they took Marie away.

We contacted Marie's friend Vicky, who then contacted Marie's younger sister, Karla. Karla arrived some days later, asked questions, and seemed satisfied that it was an accidental overdose. However, at some point, Karla, at the recommendation of Vicky, went to the Oakland Police Department and accused me of being responsible for Marie's death. I was asked to come down to the homicide department at the police station and answer questions. They told me they were investigating the death of Marie Ricks. They read me my Miranda rights and told me I didn't have to talk to them, but I wanted to talk. I told them how I had discovered Marie and they let me go; I was cleared of any wrongdoing.

I knew Karla had been coerced by Vicky, so I forgave her for going to the police. She later said to me, "I just needed some closure." Karla and I became lovers and dope partners, taking over where Marie and I had left off. Our relationship was toxic: its only foundations were dope, sex, money, and setting up her acquaintances for robberies. She set up a dope dealer in Santa Cruz. I gave her a pistol; she went inside and robbed him of about $3,000 in broad daylight. The dope dealer called the police and gave them her name and the description of the car we were driving. We didn't make it ten miles out of town before the police started chasing us, with sirens on. Before we were pulled over, I told her to hide the money in her underwear. The police, with guns drawn, said, "Get out of the car with your hands up." The money fell from her dress, and we were taken to the county jail and booked for robbery. I told them she didn't have anything to do with it, and they released her. She pleaded with my dad to bail me out, and eventually, the case was dismissed—the dealer's word and his police record were worse than mine.

The streets of Oakland flowed with Mexican brown heroin; it affected my body more than China White. I was hooked like a mad demon, always on the prowl, looking for anyone with drugs I could steal. I drove to MacArthur Boulevard in Oakland, knocked on an apartment door, walked in, pulled a gun, and robbed Clarisse B., the flunky of drug dealer Big Butt Flo. I took all the money and dope. If you rob a dope dealer in Detroit, he or she will come looking for you either to get the goods back or beat you to a pulp or kill you. They don't call the police; they handle it themselves. Word on the streets was Big Butt Flo was mad and looking for me. She told Clarisse to report the robbery to the police and to name me. Because of my multiple brushes with the law, the police knew I lived on Buena Ventura. At the door they told my dad I was a suspect in a robbery and they wanted to talk to me. He yelled, "Junior, you don't have to hide. They just want to talk to you. They ain't going to hurt you." I was thinking, "Oh my God, Dad. You weren't supposed to say I was home."

After they'd arrested me, they informed me I could pick out people for the lineup from the jail cells inside; I picked five guys who had similar noses, skin color, and height. We got our numbers and were told to line up. As soon as we started to walk in, Flo said, "That's the m— f— right there. You dirty dog."

The police officer started laughing and said, "You didn't need no lineup. She knew who you was before you even got to your number."

I was charged with armed robbery; bail was set at $50,000. Because Clarisse was an eyewitness, I was afraid a jury would convict me quickly. My dad bailed me out, and my brother-in-law Glenn came to pick me up from Santa Rita Jail. Word on the street was Flo had a hit out on me. I was as careful as I could be, but I still had to hustle to get my drugs.

After about two weeks on the streets playing the Jamaican bomb con game, I went to buy some dope from a dealer named Bugs and his girlfriend Gwen. I ordered a speedball—a mixture of heroin and cocaine. Bugs went to resupply and said it would be there any minute. In the meantime, Gwen offered to sell me some of her personal dope until

Bugs returned. I thought, "Okay." I mixed up the drugs, tied myself up, got a hit, and started to very slowly shoot the dope. All of a sudden, I felt a burning, acid-like sensation filling my veins. I yelled, snatched the needle out of my arm, and threw it on to the floor. I was sweating like someone had poured water on me, and I massaged my burning arm to get the poison out. If I had shot it quickly, I would've died on the spot. I ran out to catch some air and realized it was Flo's doing. She had paid Gwen, Bugs's girlfriend, to sell me the hot shot. I jumped in the car and went to buy some dope from Leon Jackson and told him what happened. He said, "Stay away from there, man. That broad is trying to get you."

Karla and I continued with the crime spree. One time, when we were shoplifting in Gilroy, I stayed in the car while she went in. I thought I would draw more suspicion than she would because she was White. Karla got caught by the security guard and blamed me: "The Black guy in the car outside made me do it." I called my dad and told him what happened. I said, "When I come home, I don't want her there, Dad. She lied and snitched on me." In his very kind way, he asked her to leave for the sake of peace.

My reputation as a slick manipulator continued to grow. One day Bugs, Gwen, and some of their friends were standing near their apartment. It looked to me like they were being held hostage; I saw someone with a jack handle. A big dude from upstairs had them all standing under a shed and seemed to be threatening them. As I walked over, their eyes turned toward me. Suddenly, the dude turned toward me, walked over, and pulled out a steak knife. As I turned to get out of the way, he stabbed me in the back. With all my adrenaline pumping, I didn't fall. I picked up bricks and rocks and started pounding the guy as he kept trying to hit me again with the knife. Somebody must have called the police; when they arrived, they saw me bleeding and put me in the back of the police car. When they asked who stabbed me, I said I didn't know. By this time, the guy had gotten rid of the knife. Everyone was standing on the sidewalk, which the police used as a makeshift lineup, driving me past to identify the guy. He was standing there with them in the lineup, but I said, "I don't see him."

They took me to the hospital and stitched me up. My sisters Diane and Zakiya came down to the hospital, and instead of asking me if I was alright, they were being funny, like a Black Laverne and Shirley—that's what I called them. They had me cracking up, asking if I was wearing any underwear. It hurt so bad to laugh, but I couldn't help it; all three of us were laughing out loud.

Picked up on various parole violations, I was in and out of Santa Rita for most of 1974. I made a lifelong friend while I was in Santa Rita: Jeffery Goode. We saw each other all the time as I went in and out. Jeff was a bodybuilder, and we used to work out together. Years later, in the early 1990s, when I was doing time in Avenal State Prison, Jeff got off the bus and said, "Where's John Lee Hooker Jr.?" like he was saying, "Give him a round of applause."

When he saw me, he said, "Oh, I'm going to do easy time now."

We hung out like twin brothers, always meeting after dinner, after count time, just laughing and telling jokes. I was the yard preacher in Avenal, and Jeff assisted me with my revival. We're still friends today. We text and I see him whenever I go back to Oakland to preach.

Jamie Wallace, who was also with me in the maximum-security unit called Big Greystone, in Santa Rita,[1] kept talking about how he'd put in for a change of housing. Big Greystone housed parole violators, people who had escaped before, and guys who'd committed violent crimes, like assault, rape, crimes against kids, and murders. They called Jamie's name over the speaker one day; he told me through the porthole that he was going to Superior Court Jail at Lake Merritt as the cook. I answered, "Oh my God, Jamie, you gotta pull me, homeboy."

"I'm going to try to pull you, Junior. I got juice up here." Sure enough, thirty days later, I was told to "roll 'em up," and I went to Superior Court as a trusty. It was like I'd hit the lottery. I gained so much weight. As a big bonus, my sister Zakiya was training there as a court stenographer, and sometimes I could at least see her through the door. She went on to become the head supervisor for jurors.

While I was at Lake Merritt Jail, I served the breakfast, lunch, and dinner that Jamie cooked for the inmates. One day the guard told me, "Be careful of pod A; this morning he killed his cellie. He beat him and then hanged him." When I went past his cell, the serial killer asked me very politely for an extra milk and an apple. What a psychopath—he had just killed someone twenty minutes earlier, then asked with a gentle smile if he could "please have some extras" if I had them, as though I were a waiter inside of a luxurious restaurant.

During one last time out of jail, I was arrested for jumping bail on Big Butt Flo's armed robbery charge. I was driving with the sister of my friend Tee Tee; he was my old crime partner and a master cook and thief. His sister and I were getting ready to go to a hotel room and shoot dope when we heard police sirens. I gave her the dope; she swallowed the bags so we wouldn't be arrested on a drug charge. They pulled us over and, with guns drawn, surrounded the car. We got out of the vehicle; they said, "Don't move. Keep your hands so we can see them. Down on the ground." Sister began to cry. They let her go; I was arrested and taken back to Big Greystone.

In 1975 I was convicted and sentenced for the armed robbery of Big Butt Flo. Thinking I was going to get an indeterminate sentence of five years to life because of the enhancement of having a gun during the commission of a crime, I accepted a plea deal of seven years at the California Rehabilitation Center (CRC) in Southern California. People told me I would be out in eight or nine months. I took the deal and later wished I hadn't.

# 10

# CALIFORNIA REHABILITATION CENTER

At about four o'clock in the morning, a guard awakened me: "Hooker, bag and baggage, roll 'em up. You're headed to the DOC," which was the Department of Corrections, or state penitentiary. Several of us were escorted to a holding tank and given a paper bag with a sandwich (a Christmas-tree-looking piece of meat on stale bread), a very hard cookie, and an apple for breakfast. As ironic as this may sound, I couldn't wait to get to prison to eat some better food. We were called out one by one and strip searched. Then we were chained around the waist with handcuffs and leg chains, holding our property in our hands or under our arms. I looked into the eyes of some of the men and saw fear, probably because it was their first time. I guess it wasn't that frightening to me because I had been to Wayne County Jail and Jackson Prison; maybe I was so numb or dumb that it didn't bother me that much. All state prisons are violent, corrupt merry-go-rounds. I had to be smart and protect myself: I couldn't do anything; I had to treat everyone with respect.

We were told to get on the bus and that there would be no talking while we traveled or we would be taken off the bus . . . we read between the lines: they would beat us while we were shackled if we didn't follow orders. We were quiet for ten hours. They were preventing us from conspiring to highjack the Gray Goose, as the bus was called, and escape. It was a long ride, lasting from darkness until the sun came up. After many hours of dropping prisoners off at their designated prisons, we finally arrived at CRC in Norco, Riverside County. This place was supposedly for rehabilitation. Someone who had served time there told me, "Hey Hook, wait until you get there. It's like Disneyland compared to San Quentin, Tracy, or Folsom. Just watch your back. There's a bunch of them Los Angeles Crips up in there, and they hate us 'cause we from the North."

He said there would be many homeboys from the Bay, people I'd met at Santa Rita or Superior Court Jail at Lake Merritt. The yard was full of gangbangers: the Bloods; the 415 and their founder, Mousie Brown; the Crips; the Nuestra Familia; the Mexican Mafia; and the Black Guerilla Family (BGF). I never was a gang member, but I was a sympathizer. I talked to them almost every day, laughing, exercising, and getting high. We hung out, but as far as their business meetings were concerned, I didn't indulge, and they respected that. I was the music man on the yard; I stayed away from trouble, unless the Blacks were being threatened or challenged and I had to step up.

They housed me in Dorm 11, a group-therapy unit that was legalistically strict and kept very clean. In group meetings we talked about our failures to drug addiction or alcoholism. It was straight-up fake and boring: not one of the guys in there was serious about getting clean, not even me. In fact, a brother named Stan from Fresno was one of the drug dealers in our dorm. When I finally got to the yard, my homies were waiting. Everyone hugged me, smiling as if I had just arrived home from college or a war. I had the sense they were very happy for me to be in this sugar-coated window dressing of a place filled with misery; as the old saying goes, "Misery loves company." They threw a party to celebrate my arrival. They had stolen crackers, bread, orange juice, tuna fish, onions, pickled relish, potato chips, and even meat stolen from the officer's mess. And it wouldn't have been a party without a little marijuana. Asked if I was going to start a band, I said, "Oh yeah." They introduced me to the late Calvin Boyd from Palo Alto and Kenny Love from Oakland; they had a quartet group on the yard. I also met a brother named Billy Simpson, who was in charge of recreation and had connections to the music equipment in the gym.

Lockdowns had become standard procedure due to gang warfare at CRC. One day the word came down from one of the shot callers of Nuestra Familia: a hit was going down at noon in the yard. All of us Blacks skipped our daily routine of working out that day. We watched this

Latino, who jogged every day around noontime, be rushed and stabbed by about twenty Nuestra Familia gang members until he went limp. The siren blew, and the voice over the loudspeaker said, "Lock down, clear the yard, and return to your units. Failure to do so will result in a 115 disciplinary write-up." We were locked down for one-and-a-half months, until the investigation resulting in multiple arrests for homicide was over.

The grapevine was reliable about fights: it was either the Bloods or the Crips, the Whites or the Blacks, the southern Mexicans or the northern Mexicans. Sometimes weeks would pass without violence, and then, all of a sudden, there'd be a stabbing, a fist fight, or an assault on an officer. *Boom!* Lockdown. Out of fear and a lack of solutions, the staff finally tried to bring the races together with the Ethnic Representative Committee (ERC), with reps from the Black, White, and Latino populations. Someone asked me to run as a candidate to represent the Blacks. If I won, it would be a paying job with good food and weekly meetings with the associate warden, Mr. Koehler, and possibly even a pass to fly home to seek employment. That would look really good for me at the parole board. I began campaigning immediately to become the ERC rep and won. If there was a lockdown, my job as a rep was to investigate the problem and come up with a solution to cool the flames between the rival gangs. Investigations entailed going dorm to dorm and having meetings with the shot callers. I had to be careful not to seem passive or afraid to talk to them. If I said anything that sounded like I was weak or on the police's side, I could be cursed, beaten, or stabbed and then called an informant. After some research I proposed a solution to the associate warden: these guys needed some entertainment. They were bored in this prison, with no trees or shade. I was allowed to use the phone to call the free world; I phoned theaters, dancers, and musical groups. I even called home to talk to my family.

I contacted a rock band with dancing girls and explained the problem we were facing inside the CRC. I had permission to offer them $500; they immediately agreed to perform. I had fliers made and hung all over the prison that announced a show in two months with dancing girls—provided we were all on our best behavior. Two months later, I, along with the other reps, met the group at the gate. There were three hippies and one brother with dreads—the drummer—all dressed in bell-bottoms and psychedelic shirts. Three White chicks had on skin-tight pants, turquoise necklaces, cheap beads, and platform shoes. Once they were cleared to enter the yard and set up, the girls asked where they could change into their "dance clothes." An officer escorted them to the gym, and they came back in bikinis with rhinestone bras. I said to myself, "They're going to go crazy when they see these almost-naked women, who look like they're wearing bathing suits." They sure were beautiful to anyone who had been locked up for a while. The concert was a big success; the men blew kisses, and the women blew them back. From the audience, men asked the women if they were married; some promised to get out and get a job. It was hilarious. Everyone had a ball.

The warden expressed respect for the ERC reps: "You guys are our safety measure to stop people from being killed and ethnicities from fighting each other." He asked for more suggestions; I offered a music contest. I had already started a band while in Santa Rita. I was put in charge. We had White bands, country bands, Western bands, and Mexican groups singing oldies but goodies, rock 'n' roll, and R&B. I would go around and make a list of those who wanted to audition. Some, if not most, were just terrible—I mean as bad as *The Gong Show*. I had a great blues band. I had a White keyboard player who could play anything; he was the Duke Ellington, Fats Domino, and Jerry Lee Lewis of the yard. The White boy was bad. He was so good, my dad would have hired him.

When it was almost my time for the parole board, I called my dad and asked him to do a show; I thought this could help my chances for a quicker release date. I knew the place would go crazy. It took some convincing, but I finally talked him into doing it. The anticipation was electric; this dilapidated prison had never had such a celebrity before. Four months later, the Coast to Coast Blues Band arrived with my dad. They were escorted in; my dad and I were so glad to see each other— we hugged each other real tight. My dad said, "Let's get this over with before they try and keep me in this place," and laughed. I did a couple of songs to open, and then my dad tore the place up. Men were on their feet, clapping and dancing. John Garcia was a young Mexican man who played guitar with my dad; the Latino community loved it. There was nothing but standing ovations and yelling to the delight of music.

The parole board gave me a time cut, and the associate warden gave me a forty-eight-hour pass to look for a job. I flew to Oakland; this time, I wasn't dumb enough to shoot dope; you have to test when you come back. If I had tested positive, they would've sent me to maximum security at Chino. The pass just made me want to go home even more. They then rescinded the time cut, so I had to go to the parole board on the main date. When I appeared before the board, they saw the time cut had been rescinded, checked my record, and saw that I had one minor write-up for stealing hamburgers from the officers' mess. Then I was out, after only nine months to a year at CRC. Thank God.

# 11

# ON THE RUN

I went back to Oakland and played the same con game, robbed dope dealers, boosted out of stores, and even ripped off a big-time marijuana dealer, a paraplegic who dealt out of a trailer behind a car repair shop. When the mechanic wasn't there, I went in the trailer and asked if I could buy some weed; when the dealer went to his stash, I pulled out a gun and took all the money and marijuana. I was on foot and ran three blocks, with the sack of money and the stash in a paper bag. While I was flying down the street, I heard helicopters and hid in the bushes. The guy must have dialed 911. The Oakland police had hit the air. I jumped under greasy cars and waited; finally, I made my way to the house of the dealer Leon Jackson. When I got there, I told him the police were looking for me because I broke a mark. Then I bought some dope and shot it. I knew I was in trouble—maybe facing twenty years—because I was armed, had a prior felony for the same crime, and was on parole. I gave Leon a deal on a trade of weed for some heroin, and he drove me to my sister Zakiya's house. When we got there, Leon told her the police were looking for me in a helicopter. She let me in and asked, "Boy, what you done? I know you did something."

Zakiya called my dad. When he called me, I told him I had to get out of town. The police were looking for me, and if caught, I could get twenty years. He said, "They should give you fifty," but he sent me some money anyway. After the money arrived, I took a taxi to the Greyhound station and headed to Los Angeles. Once in LA, I put my sack of clothes in a locker and headed to the 'hood on Central Avenue to cop some dope and ask if there were any con players around. I hooked up with a player named Jerky, who was from Seattle, and his brother Lowdown, a pickpocket hooked on codeine pills. They called me Magic—players never give their correct names so they can remain anonymous in case someone snitches on them. We rehearsed the con game to make sure we were in harmony with each other. We broke two or three marks that day, shot some dope, got a room, and crashed—Jerky and I laid across the bed fully dressed, and Lowdown slept on the floor. We continued playing until, one day, I overslept; they picked my pockets for the key to the Greyhound locker and stole everything I had.

I couldn't go back to Oakland because of the warrant, but I needed some help. I hit the streets and played the game solo, knowing I would be caught eventually. The one thing I didn't want to do was end up going to the Los Angeles County Jail, which is bigger than some prisons. I was a young man, and gang member convicts identify you by where you're from: coming from Oakland would mean I'd automatically be associated with the Bloods, BGF, or the 415, the enemies of the Crips. There wouldn't be too many of us down there in LA County; it's predominantly Crip world. If you're from up north, you're the enemy.

I called home later in the week and told the family I was heading to Detroit. They said, "If you get caught doing wrong, don't call here." I got high before leaving and boarded a red-eye with my cards, a fake bankroll, and a syringe full of dope tucked inside my sock. I saw a guy with a gold bracelet. Long story short, with the fake bankroll in my hand, I got him to put up the bracelet on the red-card game. I won his bracelet, and he got very angry, probably because he let a young Black dude trick him out of his jewelry. He felt like a sucker. I went back to my seat, and the man next to me was snoring. I picked his pocket and pulled out a huge stack of money that was wrapped in spreadsheets with rubber bands. I went to the bathroom to figure out where I could put all that cash; it was too much to hide in my pants pocket or shoe. I took maybe $1,500 and went back to my seat. As I was putting the rest of the money back in his sport coat, he woke up. He turned on the light and said, "You took my money. Give me my money back."

I said, "I ain't took nothing. You better wake up, buddy. You must've been drinking too much. I don't even want to sit by you no more."

I found another seat and now had two people who really hated me on that plane; it would be a long flight. And now I was nervous; if I could've jumped with a parachute, I would have. I went to the bathroom and saw the flight attendant's purse under a seat. I stole seventy dollars and went back to my seat. The flight attendant came and told me the man with the bracelet had complained that I'd stolen from him and was ready to press charges. I said, "I didn't steal nothing. We were gambling. He lost fair and square."

She said, "Sir, you aren't supposed to be gambling on this plane. That's against the law. I would suggest you give him back his jewelry."

I couldn't accept being arrested by the FBI or the marshals, so I reluctantly gave the bracelet back. Then she said, "I know it was you who stole seventy dollars out of my purse, but I'm not going to press charges." As soon as I'd landed in Dallas for what was supposed to be a quick layover, the marshals came and arrested me for gambling on the plane, a misdemeanor, and took me to Tarrant County Jail. They booked me and put me in a cell; I later learned that misdemeanor bail was set at $150, but the marshals had confiscated all of my money as evidence. After a few days in the cell, I told someone inside that, when I'd made a call to my family, no one was home and maybe they were out of the country. The truth was they had answered and told me, "We can't help you. You in Texas. We ain't coming out to get you. Do the best you can," and they hung up without saying goodbye.

When I told my dad I was in a jail in Texas, he said, "They need to give you ten years 'til you can get that dope outta your system. What they say you did?"

"Gambling," I answered.

He answered, "Trying to play the cone game."

I remember he didn't say *con*; he called it the cone game. He hung up on me a few times. Finally, I talked to a guy inside who sympathized and called his bail bondsman; he asked him to take $150 off his book to get me out of jail. It was unbelievable—he didn't even know me. When I look back over my life, I always say, "Lord, I thank you. Look where you brought me from."

I still had a stolen watch in my property, as well as a few bucks, so I went to the 'hood in Dallas, sold the watch, and shot some dope. I walked all that day and into the night and made it to a rural neighborhood; I didn't know where I was, so I threw out my thumb. I couldn't believe it when an older couple stopped for me. I told them I was headed for the bus station, and they dropped me off. I called my mother and told her I was stranded in Texas. She said, "I thought you was in jail. You ain't nothing but a big liar." They talked crazy when I was down and out, and I don't blame them. I asked her to please get me out of there. She sent

CHAPTER 11

money through Western Union and made me promise to pay back every dime as soon as I got back to California. I made it to the airport and flew back to Oakland. I couldn't go back to Detroit anymore; I felt death or prison time was waiting for me there.

I continued playing the con game, robbing, stealing, violating my parole, and being sent back to prison: I did a thirty-day, a sixty-day, a ninety-day, and a four-month stint: every time I violated parole or failed to appear, I was sent back to CRC, maybe even four or five times in one year for petty violations. I was mentally exhausted; I didn't even want to live anymore. Thinking back, I can say it's called a rehabilitation center, but nobody goes there to get rehabilitated: it was a revolving door. People go there because it's easy time: the food is good, dope is easy to smuggle inside, and/or it's near their girlfriends or their families. Nobody goes to prison to get clean and sober. The judge may say, "I'm sending you to prison, Mr. Hooker, so you can get off drugs and get into a drug program." When you get in, you think about getting good write-ups to take to the parole board and evaluation reports that say you did a great job or you stayed out of trouble; you collect them like money for good behavior, and then you go to the board. You pretend to get "rehabilitated" so you can get out and get "unrehabilitated." Trust me: real rehabilitation happens when you're just tired of being tired and you say, "Lord, help me. I can't do this anymore. I've tried and failed. Have mercy on me, Jesus." That's what happened to me.

In prison, when you're alone, you always reflect on your failures—how you've hurt the ones you love. I waited until two or three o'clock in the morning and then cried silently under my blanket, thinking about all the fun things I used to do as a boy with my little brother Robert and my sisters. I thought about going to Belle Isle Park and going swimming with our friends. I remembered that every time one of us had a birthday, my dad would take us to the 20 Grand Ballroom. I remembered going to the radio station with my dad and sitting on his lap, singing into the microphone. When the show was on, everybody back home tuned in and listened. The radio announcer said, "Here's Little Johnny Lee Hooker Jr. with his daddy, Detroit's own John Lee Hooker."

I thought about when I was a young teenager and didn't really have fun; I'd never taken a young lady to the prom. Once, I went to the movies, hoping to have sex, but I was turned down. I look back on the guys in prison who were always bragging about their baby mamas. I thank God I don't have illegitimate children all over the United States and Europe. It may sound ironic, but God used prison to keep me from danger and harm. Drugs were my romance; I didn't have time for sexual encounters. My mind was always on getting some dope to get high; that was my first priority. Sex was second—no big deal if I didn't get any. Don't get me wrong, I love romance, and I love the ladies, but I had to get that sickness off me. It sounds crazy, but I thank God for protecting me by keeping me in prison. Sometimes I would be out of jail or prison for no more than sixty days, and sometimes I'd be out for a week. One time I got out of San Quentin in the morning and went right back in that night because of a parole sweep in the Tenderloin in San Francisco.

One day a guy named Dirty Red asked me to hit a lick with him in San Francisco in the Fillmore District. We were up all night, hustling and getting loaded; after a while, we were broke and needed gas. The first person we encountered that early morning was a blind man. He heard the car and lifted his cane, calling for a taxi. We pulled over like we were the cab and said, "Yes, sir. Where would you like to go?"

He said he was going to the Golden Gate Hotel. I jumped out, and Red jumped in the backseat. I said, "Get right in, sir. No problem."

I opened the door, Red moved over to allow him to get in, and I jumped in behind him. Once we had him between us, I said, "Don't move or we'll blow your f—ing head off."

The man didn't say anything. Keep in mind, Red and I were skinny because of using dope; we must've weighed about 135 lbs., and the blind man had to be 200 lbs. The man reached his arms up as though to surrender, and we started searching his pockets. Suddenly, his arms came down around our chicken-sized necks, holding us in headlocks. He was so strong, and we were so weak; he was choking us. I told Red to let him out. Red reached over, opened the door, and he fell out of the car. He grabbed his cane and walked away fast. The blind man had whupped us. The word of God says, "Do not be deceived: God cannot be mocked. A man reaps what he sows" (Galatians 6:7).

Another time when I was with Red, we saw a guy in a military uniform hitchhiking in the Fillmore District. We stopped, asked where he was going, and offered him a ride. When we asked where was he heading, he messed up: he told us he was going to buy a car. We asked, "What kind of car are you thinking about buying, buddy?"

He answered, "Chevy or Ford—whatever my money can buy."

"How much you thinking about paying?"

"About $400 or $500."

Instantly, the Hollywood theatrics began to roll. I kicked it off; Red was able to read me and follow. While I was driving, I held Red's arm and said, "No, please, no. He's just trying to buy a car. Don't do this." Red went into his act, shaking and looking crazy. I said, "Please don't do it. Let him get his car."

The guy asked, "What's going on, man?"

I said, "He's sick. He's a drug addict. Whatever you got, give it to him, so it won't be any problem. Please." The man began to look very nervous and started to shake.

Red jerked around; the man reached in his pocket and gave us the $400 he had for the car, saying, "Here, take it. Take it."

I said to Red, "Are you okay now? He gave you the money." I pulled to the curb and told the guy to get out of the car and not look back, because I didn't want Red to shoot him. He got out of the car and hurried around the corner. No one should ever get into a dirty, smelly car with funky, rough-looking people.

At one point I tried to straighten my life out. I got a job in Oakland at ABC Security Service as a guard at a furniture warehouse. My people were proud of me, but I was still shooting dope. I was basically the fox protecting the hen house. One day, when I went to the Monroe Hotel to get loaded while in uniform—a police cap and coveralls with ABC Security—this guy asked me where I was guarding. I told him it was a place with all kinds of stuff. We developed a plan for me to let him in the gate, and he stole a bunch of merchandise. The next day, because the theft happened on my watch, I was fired—but I kept the uniform.

A friend of mine named Greg Chambers asked to borrow the uniform and cap to rob stores. With the uniform on, people trusted him. One day Greg tried to rob somebody with the uniform on, and while he was getting away, they shot him in the back, crippling him for life. But being a paraplegic didn't stop him from committing crimes; he was busted and sentenced to three years in Vacaville, a medical facility for prisoners, because of the wheelchair.

One time I was out late, around two o'clock in the morning, and it seemed like the night of the walking dead—everybody was on the streets, doing dirt. A guy named Gray Eyes walked up to me and asked if I knew where he could sell a watch; it was nice. I said I did, and he handed it over. I told him to wait right there, that I would be right back. God knows I'm not lying; I jumped and went through the side of the church where I became a minister years later. I ran in the dark, jumped fences, ended up in the East Oakland projects, and sold the watch for two bags of dope.

Sometime later I violated parole and was sent to Vacaville. Who did I run into? Gray Eyes, also in for a parole violation. I couldn't believe it: he had grown into a giant because of all of the prison food. He walked up and asked me, "Why'd you do that, man?"

I answered, "Man, you know how it is on the streets, Gray Eyes. What do I owe you?"

He said, "You owe me forty bucks. Give me two cartons of cigarettes, and we even."

Because he was in a wheelchair, I knew Greg Chambers was doing time on the blue side of Vacaville, where they had people who were already sentenced; I was on the green side, for violators en route to another prison. I sent somebody to tell Greg I was looking for him. The next day, we met at a place where we could talk for a minute. I told Greg I owed this dude two cartons of cigarettes because I had burned him on the streets and didn't want trouble. Greg said, "Don't worry about it. I got you, Junior." The next day was the store day on the blue side; Greg wheeled over and bought me two cartons. I brought Gray Eyes the cigarettes; strapped with my razor, I was ready for anything, in case he tried to bully me. He was satisfied with the two cartons but said, "My watch cost more than this twenty-five dollars' worth of cigarettes."

I told him, "The board gave me thirty days. When I get out, I'll send you the other twenty dollars." We didn't smile or anything; he just said, "Deal."

He gave me his prison number and real name. I watched my back, but he didn't want any trouble—we were both waiting to be released—he just wanted his money. As soon as I got out, I sent him a twenty-dollar money order. As a matter of fact, somebody else got out later and told me, "Gray Eyes said that was cool of you to send him the money order. Most guys wouldn't have done that." So he got the money.

Later, when Greg got out, he went back to stealing, and we hustled together. I would push him in stores and act like we were shopping. He'd take five, six, seven, and sometimes even eight pairs of Calvin Klein

or Pierre Cardin jeans and sit on them with a blanket over his legs; I
rolled him out, got him in the car, and we'd head to get loaded.

Drug addiction is of the devil. In Europe and other places, people call
liquor "spirits." I understand what they mean: the spirit of confusion,
greed, gratification—it's an awful thing. If you kill my dog, I'm going to
kill your cat. I've seen sons sell dope to their mama. I've seen daughters
sell dope to their dad and tell them, "Get off this corner. I ain't giving
you no more. Go home. I don't care if you is sick." I've seen my friend's
sister murdered because she sold her body; she'd run out the door with
the dope dealer's money and was killed. Glory to God, I'm still here to
tell this story. Jesus was my answer. He alone delivered me from the
power of the devil's addiction.

Bangor Street, Detroit, MI: John Lee Hooker and, left to right, are me, my brother Robert, and neighborhood children Fat Man and Linda, 1957.

Me, after having been released from 1300 Beaubien County Jail, with black eyes still visible and with Shyvonne (left) and Lavetta (right), 1968.

Me onstage live at Soledad Prison with Ernie, the guard, in the corner on June 11, 1972.

Me onstage at California Rehabilitation Center, 1975.

Me in boxing ring at Jamestown Conservation Camp in 1976.

Left to right: Lavetta, me, my mom, and Shyvonne at Jamestown Conservation Camp in 1976.

Me preaching at Soledad Prison Chapel in 1986.

Me as a young minister in 1987.

Me and my brother Robert in 1987.

Me, Gerry, and Jeremiah in 1989.

With my dad in 1997.

Danielle, Karen, my dad, my mom, and me in 1998.

Diane helping me at my wedding to Brenda in 1999.

Me at Grammy Awards Ceremony in 2004.

Me with Turkish gang leader Ali in 2007.

Jefferson County Texas Correctional Facility in 2009.

Me with Zakiya, onstage in Paris, in 2010.

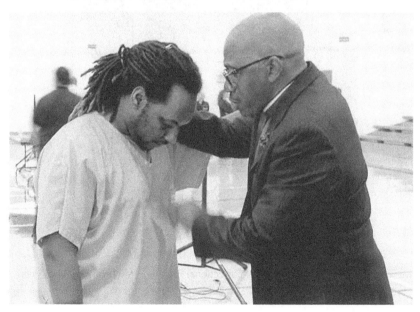

Me at Lemon Creek Prison in Juneau, Alaska, in 2012.

Me with Junior Mathis at Macomb Correctional Facility in Michigan in 2017.

Opening for the Rolling Stones at Red Bull Ring in Spielberg, Austria, in 2017.

My dad and Keith Richards in 1992.

Me and Keith Richards in 2017.

Left to right: Ronnie Wood, Keith Richards, me, Mick Jagger, and Charlie Watts in 2017.

With my mother during filming of the video for "My God Is Holy," 2017.

With my wife, Birgit, in 2018.

Left to right: Me, Pastor Andreas Pauly, and Pastor Heinrich Paster of the Evangelisch Church of Cloppenburg, Germany, in 2023.

Left to right: Parviz Mir-Ali (composer/producer), Rev. Imke Leipold, Rev. John Lee Hooker Jr., Rev. Andreas Leipold, Rev. Fabian Vogt, and Rev. Dieter Dersch in 2024.

# 12

# BACK IN CRC, SOLITARY AT CHINO, AND GILROY

Eventually, I was sent back to CRC. After about a month, I became the new cameraman, taking photos inside the visiting room and on the yard. It was a cool job; I got to see all the pretty women come and visit other inmates. I became the man who could carry drugs to the population without being thoroughly searched. Inmates called me over to their table and asked for a photo; at the same time, they'd pass me the dope. I got paid after visiting; they gave me a cut.

At some point in 1976, my dad moved from the Bay Area down to Gilroy, the garlic capital of the world. It reeked of garlic in the summer and made your stomach hurt, especially if you were dope sick. Before I got out, he told me over the phone, "Man, they got pretty women out here! I got two of 'em living here, and they clean up the house and cook for me, he, he, he."

As the cameraman, I'd had my picture taken for free. Now that I was heathy, I sent photos to my family in Oakland and Detroit and to my dad in Gilroy. He showed the photos to the ladies in the house, and I was instantly an infamous, attractive, coveted player. Inside, I knew I was still a snake. I couldn't wait to get out and be with a woman. My dad said to me one day, "Boy, they waiting on you. Now, when you get out, Junior, play your music or travel with me. Man, quit wasting all that talent, and leave the dope alone, or they gonna send you right back to dem places, and you know how much you hate being there. They ain't got no girls in there, do they?"

I answered, "No, Dad."

Then he said, "Okay, get out here, and do the right thing."

I answered, "Dad, you crazy."

One time when I called home, he said, "Somebody want to speak to you. She want yo address so she can write you. Her name is Diane. Boy, she pretty too."

When I got out, there was a party at my dad's house. His band was there, and his new neighbors, some store and bar owners, people who worked for the city, and so many pretty women—my age, younger, and older—all competing for me, especially Lenora, Diane, and Vicky. Diane said, "My room is next door to yours." Lenora's room was at the end of the hall. I had choices. I settled for Lenora after Diane, if you know what I mean.

After living in Gilroy for a while, I learned who the heroin dealers were. I also became acquainted with the narcotics squad: Huerta and his deputy—Batman and Robin. They hated me. Every time they saw me riding in my Cadillac with women who weren't Black, they knew I was high and pulled me over, checked my eyes, and took me to jail for being under the influence. This went on for several months, until I was arrested for armed robbery. The word of God says, "For the love of money is a root of all kinds of evil" (1 Timothy 6:10). I was hooked enough to play the con game solo in a small town, where no Black people lived—my dad and I were the only Black men living in Gilroy in 1976. One day I was sick, drove up to a gas station attendant in a booth; flashed my fake bankroll of $25,000; and spoke with a South African accent to play the con game. The attendant emptied the cash register. I used the knot to pull the usual switch. After I drove off, something inside my head said, "You a fool. He gonna scream bloody murder as soon as he opens that knot, sees that Gilroy newspaper instead of cash, and finds out he's been tricked. He gonna be upset because he'll lose his job."

I fled to East Oakland to get some dope. After a few days, I returned; my dad said the police had been there, looking for me. A lion or a bear always returns to the exact place where he's peed and left his scent: there I was, back in the same place, high as a kite. Seeing the familiar car outside, Batman and Robin knocked on the door. I ran and hid under the bed. I began wondering, "Why is it taking my dad so long to say, 'He's not here?'" The next thing I knew, my dad was down on his knees, telling me to come out, assuring me the police just wanted to ask a few questions. The police arrested me and took me in for 211 PC, armed robbery. The gas station attendant was too embarrassed to say he was tricked with an accent and a fake bankroll. He said I robbed him with a knife. While my dad was away, the police kicked in the door, searching for evidence to use against me. They ransacked the place and found a small folding Buck knife.

My family got me an attorney named Dennis, who asked if I had an encounter with the guy.

I said, "Yeah, I played him."

He asked, "What do you mean?"

I told him I'd played the con game and ran it down for him. Dennis told me, "The station attendant says you pulled out a knife, opened it, twirled it around to scare him, and he gave you all the money in the cash register."

I told him that was a lie. Dennis said, "Let's see what happens." We got to court, and the district attorney and the deputies were acting like they hated my guts. I told Dennis, "Man, those are some racist people." Dennis agreed, just like that. I was afraid I was going to get railroaded. I didn't actually rob the guy; I tricked him out of the money. After we went through the pretrial and chose the jury, I told Dennis I didn't trust the court system. I asked him to see if the district attorney (DA) would make a deal. The DA looked at Dennis and me and said, "Eight years, or let the chips fall where they may." Well, that's the max, so I went ahead with the trial because I wasn't guilty of armed robbery, and they were racist. It was the only time I ever went to trial. I had my yellow pad in front of me and assisted my attorney with questions.

The kid testified that I twirled the knife around in my right hand, told him to give me the money, and, with the same hand, closed the knife and put it back in my pocket. He said I drove off afterward. I wrote notes while he testified. The knife had a locking mechanism in the middle: it wasn't possible to fold it with one hand. When it was time for the cross examination, while holding the knife, Dennis asked the kid to show him how I did it. The kid said he didn't know how. So Dennis said, "Let me show you. For me to fold this knife with my right hand would be impossible because, ladies and gentlemen of the jury, it has a lever switch that requires two hands," and he showed the jury and passed it around.

The cross-examination caught the guy in so many lies. The trial lasted two days and then went to the jury. Back in the courtroom, the judge asked, "Ladies and gentlemen of the jury, have you reached a verdict?" "Yes, we have, your Honor."

They gave the judge the paper, then he gave it back: "We, the jury, find the defendant, John Lee Hooker Jr., not guilty of 211 PC, armed robbery. We, the jury, find the defendant guilty of misdemeanor petty theft." When the judge polled the jury, they said they didn't believe I was guilty of armed robbery but thought I must have done something. I was relieved, but it still meant I had to go back to prison.

By this time I was sick of being sent back to CRC. One time while I was there, I was so burnt out that I refused to work, go along with the program, or see my counselor. I was sent to "segregation"—the hole in Chino. It was a disciplinary action for insubordination and aggressive behavior, although the violation was really for my loud voice and refusal to work. It was close to one hundred degrees in that small cell—eight to ten feet long by four feet wide—with no activities: I was locked down twenty-three hours a day, alone, but I could hear everything. There was no fan in that heat, and showers were once a week, or I could wash up in my cell sink. After about two weeks, they escorted me to a room where I was read my disciplinary action. I admitted I was guilty of having a bad temper and refusing work duties. They asked if I was ready to return to the program at CRC or if I wanted to spend the rest of my time, six months, at Chino. I chose to go back rather than die by suffocation inside that hole.

# 13

# BOXING AT CONSERVATION CAMPS

In 1976 or 1977, I was sentenced to sixteen months to two years at Jamestown Sierra Conservation Center, where they train inmate firefighters. Once there, I inquired about people on the yard from the Bay Area. I learned that Rubber Duck, Bowlegged John, Spicy Mike, and Drexel (the shot caller from CRC) were there. Jamestown had the Mexican Mafia, Nuestra Familia, Arian Brotherhood, 415, Black Guerilla Family (BGF), Crips, and Bloods. A BGF shot caller had slipped through the cracks of security and was on the adjoining yard. Normally, high-profile gang members aren't allowed to go to camp, but some get there undetected, while others are put there on purpose—for example, if they have decided to quit their gangs and are scared for their lives. I wasn't a gang banger, but the "car" from the Bay Area would always have my back if anything should happen. One thing about prison is you don't ever want to be a lone person on the yard, not knowing anyone. But my things were boxing, exercising, music, and the stage.

I moved into a dorm with a Louisianan from Oakland named Larry Areo. Larry worked in the kitchen as an officer's cook and always tried to please Tony, the Puerto Rican cartel-type dealer so he could get high every weekend. Larry would bring Tony breakfast in bed straight from the kitchen every morning. Larry, Tony, and the gang leader, named Ernesto, were hooked on heroin. Tony was a cool guy, but after a while, I began to put two and two together: "Why is this big cartel dealer in a level-one camp, and why is he getting this gang leader dope every week?" My two and two added up to he'd probably told on someone in the cartel, and they'd sent him there for protection. One day the BGF leader, Puerto Rican Tony, said to me, "Do you get high, Hooker?"

"Oh, yeah," I said.

He said, "Me and you, next week, homeboy. You a really cool brother, plus I like your style; you're quiet and not like the others. You don't sweat nobody. Just hit one of those songs when we get high, cool?"

"No problem." Every time he'd get his dope, I would smoke some weed; every now and then, he'd offer me some heroin. He would say, "Hit one for me, Hooker." I would sing Jimmy Reed's "Baby What You Want Me to Do." He loved it, saying it was one of his favorites.

We went through classification and training, and for some reason, they just kept putting mine off. In the meantime, I met Buddy Miles, Jimi Hendrix's former drummer, who was in for running a stolen car ring—or so he said. Buddy was a very talented individual, and every musician there knew it, even the jealous inmates. Buddy didn't talk like he was from the 'hood; he talked like a White college boy, always saying, "Yes, sir," or "Yes, ma'am," and "How is your day so far?" When he said, "Good morning," people answered, "What's good about it?" Passive and soft-spoken, he walked with a wobble because he was an obese dude: he wore giant prison jeans and size four or five extra-large T-shirts. Inmates teased him about the way he talked and his size. It's sad to say, but Buddy wasn't very hygiene-minded; they made jokes about his unkemptness and sometimes cursed at him, but people would give him his props when we were together. They also gave him his creds when they heard the big man on those drums. I liked Buddy a lot, and it was a good thing he was in prison camp—San Quentin, Tracy, and Folsom weren't good places for a man like Buddy Miles.

We formed a blues band. Buddy could sing like Sam and Dave, and he hit everything. In addition to drums, we had guitar, bass, saxophone, and keyboard; the whole staff would come when we gave a show. We did John Lee Hooker, of course, and B. B. King. One guard asked, "What are you guys doing here? You should be out in Las Vegas." You could have taken that band to the Chicago Blues Festival and wowed the crowd.

I was eventually excluded from firefighting for medical reasons I lied about, and then I was assigned light duty: cleaning the dorm. When the guys went to work, I'd go have fun: smoke some weed, run, hit the bag, and train. The stage was also the boxing ring. After Slim Goody started me fifteen years earlier, I'd kept at it. There was a heavy bag at CRC, and during sixty days spent at Vacaville in quarantine, I trained with a guy named Rock. He called me The Hook. At Jamestown I worked out and hit the heavy bag every day. I was in good shape: I ran six miles every other day and lost weight. This old guy named Preacher Martin, from San Francisco, came up one day and said, "Homeboy, you can throw them things. Let me train you."

I trained under Preacher Martin for about four months and would spar with different dudes in my weight class; sometimes I trained with heavyweights, and my ribs got bruised. I learned very quickly how to protect my rib cage. Word got out that I could chunk 'em; I was challenged and whupped a bunch of guys in there.

A recreation staff member told us the boxing team from the nearby town of Tracy wanted to challenge a boxer from each weight class inside the prison. There were five or six of us in serious shape and who were considered pretty good boxers. At 160 lbs., I was chosen for my class—middleweight. We couldn't wait to beat up a free person from the streets. I trained my butt off because I knew if I got beat up, I would be considered a sissy and clowned every time I looked up.

The Tracy team showed up with an attitude: swagger and no smiles; they looked at us like we were nothing, like a bunch of thugs and dope addicts who'd robbed society. The first lightweight prisoner, Floco, knocked the Tracy fighter out in the first round. The convict audience went berserk, yelling, "Take that ass back home, dude." Then the next prison fighter, Kenyatta, won. And then the next. My homies from the Bay Area were waiting for me. My Tracy fighter had long hair, like a hippie; when he stepped into the ring, the inmates began to whistle and cat call, saying, "Hey baby, what's your name?" The fighter was so mad—you could see in his eyes he wanted to destroy me and shut up the big fat mouths of the convicts.

The bell rang, and I heard them: "Knock his ass out, Hook." It was a first-round technical knockout: I kept slipping his jab and countering with my own. I went to the body a few times to set him up, then went for the knockout and missed by inches. The whole gym said, "Ohhhh!" Being worn down by the body punches and feeling the wind of my blow pass inches from his face, the Tracy fighter began to run around the ring. I chased him with my fist jokingly in the air; the gym went crazy with laughter. His dad was the referee and got so infuriated, he said, "Fight me, you SOB!" Two of the inmates got inside the ring and said,

"You don't want none, old man." He comforted his son as he removed his gloves.

At Jamestown there was a White guy named Elvis Presley who was a boxer. He had pitch-black hair and walked with a swagger; he always had two or three guys with him everywhere he went. I saw him training and instantly said to myself, "I will tear his head off if we ever get into the ring." When he was sparring, he looked out of the ring at me like, "You want some of this?" I really liked Elvis; his pretension to be a tough guy made me laugh, so I always smiled and told his crew, "He don't want none of this. I will knock him to the canvas."

Elvis boxed without anticipating where the fist would come back at him after he'd thrown his, like he was street fighting. I had the edge on him. One day the challenge came; instigators provoked Elvis to call me out. It was not a racial callout—but for most of the yard, it was a challenge about the sets we were from, our races, especially because his name was Elvis Presley and mine was John Lee Hooker Jr.—rock 'n' roll against the blues. A yard artist made a flier picturing Elvis Presley, coming in with an upper cut with one hand and a guitar in his other hand, and me, ducking with an overhand and holding a microphone in my other glove. It said, "John said he's going to give him the blues. Elvis said he's going to rock his world." The fight was called The Jail House Rock. Promotion for the fight was unbelievable.

There was dope being bet, as well as cash, cigarettes, and food; I believe even the guards were betting. But when the week of the blockbuster fight came, I was rolled up for camp. I now believe they shipped me out because they knew that if I'd knocked out Elvis Presley, there would've been violence on the yard. It happened too quickly. Lying rumors spread among some, like, "Hooker asked to be shipped to camp, asked to be rolled up. He was afraid a White boy named Elvis Presley would embarrass him when he whupped Hook's ass." It was hilarious—I almost cried when they told me I was shipping out. Boxing was fun: you train, you discipline yourself, and you quit smoking, at least until the fight is over.

I was sent to Growlersburg Conservation Camp 33 in Georgetown and was never called to fight a fire; I was the dorm trusty with light duty. While everyone was at a fire or doing preventative work, like making fire lines, I was in the little fitness spot. Camp 33 was so kicked back, they called it Disneyland; it had the best food for a prison camp, plus guys stored food in their lockers that their families brought them during visits. We smoked weed there like it was legal; Whites, Blacks, and Latinos hung out and got high together. I liked not having to watch my back. There was not a thought about rehabilitation, therapy, or any concern about my drug habit when I hit the streets.

It was during my time at Growlersburg that I started hearing about the Lord Jesus Christ; my newly converted ex-crime partner—my brother, Robert—sent me letters once every two weeks. While I was in prison, Robert had gone back to Detroit and, to my surprise, converted to an apostolic church where some believe that to enter into the Kingdom of Heaven, you must speak in tongues by being filled with the Holy Ghost. I believe my younger brother was turned radical by some of the church doctrine. Late in life, he came to himself and learned the truth: "For it is by grace you have been saved, through faith—and this is not from yourselves, it is the gift of God—not by works, so that no one can boast" (Ephesians 2:8-9).

On every letter he drew a picture of a devil, and the fires of hell on every envelope; the cartoon images actually frightened me. He would say, "Junior, you are going to burn in hell if you don't accept Jesus Christ into your heart and be filled with the Holy Ghost and speak in tongues! Don't mess with any other church, or you will join the devil's church."

I was scared for him; I thought, "What is this? Is he telling me the truth? Which way do I go?" I must admit I hated getting mail from my brother and thought, "The boy done went crazy. I don't want to join his church."

This went on for eight months; I decided that when I got out, if I did go to a church, it would not be an apostolic one. Now as I look back, I see Robert had a zeal, but not according to knowledge. Still, he planted a seed in my spirit as the deacon Stephen did to the apostle Paul (Acts 7:55-56); later Paul was converted by the Lord Jesus Christ on the road to Damascus.

# 14

# THE CON IN DETROIT
## I'M SHOT

By the time I got out of Growlersburg, the Monroe Hotel had been shut down; I rode past it one day, and it was still there but boarded up. With the Monroe closed, I was homeless. In 1981 I went back to Detroit and learned it was more dangerous than California—deadlier. In California you could sell dope on the street corner; in Detroit, you had to do it in a house because there were robberies. Houses had peepholes and beams of wood across the door, and everyone was armed.

I stayed with Big Mama, hooking up with some people from my childhood and from the streets and bringing the con game from California to the East Side of Detroit. Most days I left Big Mama's with a newspaper, a deck of cards, three tops and a pea for the greasy pig, a mish, and a knot—always ready to attack the minute I saw an opening on a sucker. Big Mama would ask, "Where you going, Junior?"

I'd say, "I'm going to work, Big Mama."

"Where? You ain't got no job, boy. You better be careful out there. Dem folks will kill you, Junior."

"I'll be alright, Big Mama."

With a newspaper under my arm, I said to the first mark that I encountered, "Excuse me, but have you seen this before? I can't gamble you nothing, but I can give you a free demonstration. Do you got good eyes? I noticed you don't wear glasses. Show me where the red card is." And he picked the card.

I said, "If I would've bet you ten bucks, you wouldn't have found it."

The mark answered, "Oh, yes, I would've."

I said, "Hold on, money on the wood makes the bet good. Put your money up." And then I let him win the ten dollars.

Then I asked, "Was that a lucky guess, or you knew it all the time? Am I too slow?"

He answered, "You a little bit slow." I played him from there. After I won, I shook his hand and said, "That was a fair game." Then I headed off to the dope house to feed the devil's habit.

I ran into an old childhood friend, lil' Junie, who was on dope, like me. One day as I was coming out of the shooting gallery, Junie told me someone was looking for me. As he was warning me, a couple of guys approached me; one had a .38 caliber pistol pulled out.

Junie said, "Johnny, run! Here they come."

As they chased me with the gun, I ran, jumped a fence into someone's yard, and came out on the side of another house. I decided I wouldn't run anymore. I was very nervous and hoped I could maybe talk my way out of it. As I walked toward the potential killers with my hands raised, I heard Junie say, "Johnny, no, run. Johnny, run, man!" When one of the men pointed a gun at my face, I said in a loud voice, "So, you gonna kill me in front of all these people?"

He looked at the crowd watching, stared at me for about twenty seconds, and reluctantly put the pistol back in his pants, saying, "I ought to kill you, m— f—. Take your ass back to the 'hood you came from, nigga." Then they left.

Junie said, "Johnny, man, you crazy. Them dudes are fools. You could've been killed. Let's go."

Sometime later, on the first of the month (when disability checks were distributed), I saw a lady coming down from Jefferson Street, and I shook the red card with her. I baited her with the fake bankroll, giving her the impression she could win more than the $800 she already had. Long story short, I let her win a couple of times, then bent the red card and purposely fumbled it so she could see the winning card was bent. She bet the $800—all that was in her purse. When she turned over the card and saw it was black, she said, "No, please give me the money. I got to feed my kids."

I said, "Ma'am, you lost fair and square." I called a taxi, went to get some cocaine and heroin, and headed to the shooting gallery. It was a good afternoon for me—or so I thought.

Here's me, the big dummy: I went back to the shooting gallery on the same street where I broke the lady for every dime she had. I knocked on the door, and everybody was sitting nervously and quietly at the table. When I walked in, there was a guy standing behind the door; he shut it, pointed his .38 at me, and told me to give his wife's money back.

I said, "Man, I ain't took no money."

"Give me my wife's money," he answered, "or I'm going to blow your brains out."

I said, "I swear to God, I ain't got no money."

*Pow!* He shot me in the upper thigh, and I fell to the floor—two or three inches higher, and I couldn't have fathered my son. Then he pulled the trigger back and aimed it at my head. I acted like I was crying: "I swear to God, I don't have nothing. Do you think I would die over $800?" He threatened to blow my brains out again; I covered my head with my hand as he aimed the gun. He hit me with the gun and broke my hand; then he ran out the door. He was frightened somebody might have heard the shot. He turned before leaving and said, "I should've killed your punk ass."

I got up, hopped out of the room, and knocked on the next-door neighbor's door; I didn't want to shoot dope in that place in case he came back—I still had the money in my pocket. When the neighbor let me in, I asked for a cooker and water and shot my dope. But I didn't get high, because of the adrenaline. I bet God just shook his head and said, "You're about the dumbest man I know." Someone called an ambulance. They came and took me to Receiving Hospital. The bullet had gone through my upper thigh; my hand was fractured, and they put it in a cast. Big Mama came to see me and said, "Junior, you got your mama and your daddy scared to death. They worried about what you done did. Your daddy said you tricking people out of they money. Boy, they going to kill you. I bet you got shot because you was messing with one of them young heifers. I know I shouldn't have let that heifer in here the other day." She always called women heifers. But I hadn't been messing with anyone.

After I left the hospital, I was sore, limping with a crutch, and had a cast on my hand. I went with Big Mama to cash a check on Belvedere and Mack Avenues so she could shop for groceries, and we ran into the guy who'd tried to kill me in front of the crowd. He looked at me and said, "You ain't dead yet?" I thought to myself, "How cruel."

It seemed almost everyone I grew up with had become dope addicts or prostitutes. Some were murdered, some had overdosed, and others had died of AIDS. Detroit had become the murder capital of the world. There were no more cashmere coats, alligator shoes, or processed hair—none of that. I hooked up with a guy I'd grown up with, Billy Wine. We called him that because he drank wine and shot dope together to enhance his high. He was living in an abandoned house like a fugitive because everyone was looking for him. Billy was dirty, like Dirty Bob and Dirty Red—and I could put myself in that category too. They caught Billy on Mack Avenue and blew his brains out; there was no investigation. With the way I was living on the streets, I became afraid for my life.

The book of Jeremiah says, "Can people change the color of their skin or a leopard it's spots? Neither can you do good who are accustomed to doing evil" (13:23). I was in the same old rut. After being nursed back to somewhat good health, I hooked up with Shirley Mathis, my cousin—Junior Mathis's older sister (he was back in prison for nine years). I continued with my ways. When I was so dope sick that I didn't have the patience to fix a knot and a mish and look for a mark, I robbed. I would shoot dope with Shirley and her boyfriend. He tried to control her and could be violent. Of course, I had a violent streak in me too. I was raised to take up for my relatives and defend them by any means necessary. Shirley would often talk to me about her boyfriend: "Cuz, I love him. Don't bother him. He loves me too." Her boyfriend felt I was a threat and didn't want me around. He told Shirley to tell me to go back to the East Side.

I heard Shirley tried to shake the relationship; the guy would beat her and keep her out every night, away from her baby girl, Tavia. Aunt Lois used to tell her, "He ain't no good for you. Leave that dirty m— f— alone, or one day he gone kill you, Shirley Ann!"

Shirley came home early one morning after running away from her crazy boyfriend, and he came looking for her. Somehow he got into the house and came up toward Shirley's bedroom with a rifle. Aunt Lois stopped him in the stairwell and told him, "Get out of my house, n—, or I'm calling the police!"

He demanded Shirley come with him. Auntie said, "She ain't here. Now get out of my house!" And she grabbed the front of the rifle. He shot her in the chest, and she died right there on the stairs.

Shirley's boyfriend was now on the run, and my Uncle Nig was paranoid he would come back and either kill the witnesses or try to kidnap Shirley again. He asked me and some other relatives to come over and help him guard the house. When I arrived, he gave me a .25 caliber pistol. I was dope sick; my first thought was "How much money can I get for this?" I know Uncle Nig probably said to himself, "I better get that pistol from Junior Hooker 'cause he'll ease out the door and sell it for drugs." I was waiting a little bit longer for the right time to get out the door, jump down the street, get over to Mack Avenue, and sell the pistol, but Uncle Nig took it back before I could do that. At daybreak I left the house on the hunt.

After my Aunt Lois's death, Shirley went deeper into her addiction and, not too many years later, died of a dope-related health problem. The last time I saw her, her hands, feet, and legs were swollen with abscesses. She was my partner; she would say, "I love me some Junior Hooker."

With all she went through, it's a miracle Shirley's daughter, Tavia, grew up to be a beautiful woman of faith. Thank God she didn't follow in her mother's footsteps.

All the deaths, the overdoses, and the violence made me ask myself, "What will happen to me if I keep up this destructive lifestyle?" But I shut out the thought of being killed in the streets, overdosing, or going to prison for the rest of my life. I was in denial. I told myself, "It won't happen to me. It hasn't happened yet."

Fast-forward many years, when I was clean and sober and a chaplain, I flew to Michigan from California to see Junior Mathis, who was doing life at Macomb Correctional Facility for murder. One day he told me he'd gone to breakfast and sat down at the table right across from the man who had killed his mama. They recognized each other. Junior told me, "He was sitting across from me, and there was nothing I could do. He was sickly, and so was I. Neither one of us could fight." They never saw each other again. They both died in prison.

I thought to myself, "Two killers sitting across from one another; one killed the other's mother, and the other killed a mother's son." Job says, "As I have observed, those who plow evil and those who sow trouble reap it" (4:8).

Finally, I decided to leave Detroit. I called home, and Big Mama helped me, telling my family, "Next time, they gonna kill him for playing them tricks on people. Y'all better get this boy out of Detroit fo' he be dead." The family relented but said, "We will help you get back, but you got to find somewhere else to live."

I said, "No problem."

I boarded the red-eye and, not caring about what had happened before, I gambled and won, without anyone reporting me to the attendants. I was relieved to have money for dope when I returned.

**4**

# REDEMPTION
# AND FALLS

# 15

# BACK IN OAKLAND, I TURN TO THE LORD

In Oakland I went back to the same old thing: I hooked up with various street people and con players, like Killer Son, Mellow Mel, Bowlegged John, and Red Card Dave; we spent many years together, doing time in and out of Santa Rita County Jail. With nowhere to go, I walked the streets, broke people, took their money, and ran and hid, knowing that if I got caught, I could be killed. One time, after staying up for several nights, I was broke and exhausted, so Bowlegged John and I broke into an abandoned room at the Aztec Hotel on Eighth Street. We were so tired, we slept on a dirty mattress. The next day it was back to the same thing: I went to Old Man's Park in Oakland, took codeine, drank wine, and hit the streets again. Another time, my sister Karen got a call from her girlfriend, who said I fell out; she'd seen me on my knees, leaning on a pole, passed out on Seventy-Third Avenue and Foothill Boulevard. I don't remember anything, but Karen told me she jumped in her car, rode to the corner, got me up and into the car, and drove me back to her place in Oakland. She loved me, but she put me in the garage so I couldn't steal from her. The next morning I woke up and asked, "How'd I get here?" She told me the story, and I thanked her, but I headed right back out to the streets.

One day I was arrested for a traffic warrant and had cocaine in my sock. The cop asked for my ID; I told him I didn't have one and gave a fake name. The police ran my plates and arrested me. In his superficial search, the officer missed the cocaine. If he missed it again, I would take it to jail, sell some, and get high. They found it downtown: the thirty days I received for a traffic fine became one year in Santa Rita Jail.

---

CHAPTER 15

After serving six months at Santa Rita, I was released for a work furlough in Oakland. I wanted to get a job, a place to live, stay off dope, and hopefully find a beautiful lady to spend my life with and build a family. Someone from Santa Rita told me about a construction job that paid ten dollars per hour in cash under the table. I got the job and lived at a halfway house.

On my way to work on the first or second day, I was transferring busses and saw this fine White girl with fire-engine red hair, maybe thirty years old, at the bus stop. My instincts and adrenalin kicked in, and I said, "Hey, Red," like I knew her. I could tell I startled her; it was seven o'clock in the morning, not quite daylight. She said, "My name isn't Red."

I said, "Please forgive me. I do apologize. What is your name?"
She said, "Julie."
"That's such a pretty name. I bet you hear that a lot."
"No, it's been a long time since somebody said that."
I said, "My name is John Lee."
Her bus was coming, so I said, "Please, please, please give me your number. I promise not to abuse it." When she asked for mine, I told her I could only give her a pay phone number.

She looked me up and down and said, "Well, you don't look like you're a bad guy. Here you go."

I said, "Julie, you made my day. Will you be catching the same bus tomorrow?" She said, "Yes, and you?"

"Oh, yes, and trust me, I will never miss a bus again for the rest of my life."

Julie was from Dubuque, Iowa, and had decided to try California. She was living with friends in the projects in Oakland and working in a glass factory in East Oakland.

The next time I saw her, I asked if she had a boyfriend, and she said, "No, I got this guy. He likes me, but . . . ." Pretty soon he was out of the picture. I gave her an ultimatum: "It's either him or me."

I called her every day from the pay phone at the halfway house and told her my story; I explained, "I'm not like that no more. I'm not my past; I'm my present." She was a country girl: straight as an arrow, no drugs, nothing—a square. She said, "I must be crazy. A guy who was in jail walks up to me at the bus stop and calls me Red."

Because I had to be back at work furlough at certain times, we met at lunch break or when she was off. Eventually, she came to see me at the halfway house—all the guys, who were peeping through the blinds as she came up, started congratulating me. When I got an eight-hour pass, I used it to be with her. Before we got a room for the first time, she said she needed something: a condom and a small bottle of Smirnoff Vodka. She said she needed the drink because she couldn't do this sober. I busted up laughing, and so did she.

I was finally released, and we moved into an apartment together. As time passed I fell back into my old ways—using dope and breaking into anything that had a lock on it. I tried to do the right thing, but right wasn't in me; I didn't have the power to do right. I realized I needed help, but where could I find it? She would put me out, let me back in, and then put me out again; she didn't like it, and I don't blame her. I went back to the con game and drugs, and she got pregnant.

Finally, I was arrested in late 1984 for grand theft: breaking a priest in a con game. A guy called Money and I spotted a priest coming out of a Catholic church and had an idea where he might be going: to drop off the collection. We broke him on the trust game and got all the money in the same way we manipulated everyone else. He went to the police and, rather than lie and say he was robbed because he was too embarrassed to admit he'd been fooled, he was honest and admitted he was scammed like a fool. They showed him vice books with con players, and he picked me out. When I got to Oakland City Jail, I was sick as a dog but then saw Kiki, a con player I knew. The first thing Kiki asked was "You sick?"

I said, "Hell, yeah."

"I got some dope." It was late when Kiki popped open the bag and poured it on some paper. Of course, we didn't have needles in there, so we snorted it. What a relief!

I got to Santa Rita the next day, and the sickness came back. I entered my plea and was waiting for sentencing, ready to get it over with. Back in Santa Rita, I met up with con players I'd worked with in Oakland and San Francisco. I got settled into my dorm; Red Card Dave gave me some soups and candy bars. I was lying there, sick and drained from running the streets, when I heard the bell for chapel. Dave said, "Come on, Hook. Might be some church women up in there. Let's go catch us one."

I was so sick and tired; reluctantly, I walked to the chapel with Dave and a couple of other gang members. We all went in; Missionary Yancy was there but, to their disappointment, no pretty women. Missionary Yancy said, "Bow your head." She talked about God and, at the end, she said something that turned my whole life around: "If there's any one of you who is tired of being tired, and you've tried everything—you've been to drug programs, you've been to jail. If you've tried everything and nothing worked, try Jesus Christ. Won't you come?"

Nobody moved. I heard guys saying, "I didn't come to no jail to get weak." But I stood up with tears in my eyes. She asked, "Young man, are you ready to try Jesus Christ?"

I said, "Yes, ma'am."

She said, "Raise your hands to heaven." I raised my hands to heaven and closed my eyes, and she led me to Christ. She said, "First, you have to acknowledge and confess that you are wrong, that you've been running all your life—running from the Lord Jesus Christ."

I said, "Yes, I've been running." She asked me my name, and I said, "Hooker."

She continued, "Brother Hooker, you've been running. I can tell you've been running. Are you tired?"

"Yes, I'm tired."

"Are you ready to accept Jesus Christ?"

I confessed I was a sinner in need. I believe that the seed my brother had planted finally sprouted. He always said, "All you have to do is believe in Jesus Christ, believe God raised Him from the dead, and you'll be saved."

I said, "I believe it." I believed there was a God back then like I do right now. I had been to so many drug programs: Synanon, Bridge over Troubled Waters in Berkeley, CRC, Napa Methadone, programs in San Francisco (Haight Ashbury), and outpatient programs with packets of pills. I had been to twelve-step programs: "Hi, my name is Johnny, and I'm alcoholic. I'm a dope fiend." I had shock therapy and saw a psychiatrist. Nothing worked; I was a slave to the devil, but I hadn't hit rock bottom yet. In the church in Santa Rita Jail, everything just came in on me; I threw my hands in the air and said, "Lord, have mercy on me. I'm tired of running."

Red Card Dave, Rubber Duck, and all the thugs were looking at me. She said, "Young man, you just continue to come. I believe God saved you." I left, knowing a miracle had occurred in my life in that instant. I was at the lowest point in my life: withdrawing from drugs, standing at a crossroad, and not knowing which way to go. It was a moment of surrender—not like when you come out to the police with your hands up—this was a surrender to trusting that there was an entity that would take my soul and protect me. I felt relief because I believe the spirit of

God had answered me, telling me, "I hear you. You now belong to me." I felt accepted.

Missionary Yancy came back in two weeks, and I was there. She gave me a card with an address for a shelter she had that helped people who were homeless when coming out of prison. I knew God had touched me and saved me. Every time I heard the chapel bell, I was there with my Bible. I wrote home to say I'd accepted the Lord Jesus Christ into my life. My family believed it because I'd quit smoking and cursing. This is where the miracle happened.

My two to three years for grand theft eventually turned into sixteen months, and I was offered a choice between Tracy Farm, Tehachapi, and Soledad; I chose Soledad, where my dad and I had performed in 1972.

I got reacquainted with the guard Ernie, who was on the side of the stage during the show. Then I got settled and started my landscape job. Soon I asked where the chapel and band room were. I went to the rehearsal room and recognized someone from the streets. One day, when I'd been out hustling solo in San Francisco, I met a guy named Gene, who I later learned was a saxophone player. We struck up a conversation: he told me he was waiting for a pawn shop to open. I asked what he was selling, and he pulled out a man's diamond watch. I said I may know someone who would buy it. I grabbed it out of his hand and ran. At that moment, there was a milk truck turning the corner, and Gene was chasing me, so I jumped on the back of the truck. I jumped off at the Bay Area Rapid Transit (BART) station and headed to Oakland.

I wanted to sell the watch and knew I could get $800 or $900 for it, but I didn't want to go to a pawn shop. I went to Bugs's place to sell it for dope. Bugs wasn't there, but that girlfriend who'd given me the hot shot, Dirty Gwen, was. I told her I was looking to sell the watch, and she said she knew where to go. We walked over to a big dope dealer's house, and she told me to give her the watch. I said, "Oh, no."

She said, "He won't let you in, John Lee." The dealer had a gate and buzzed people in. To make a long story short, she burned me. She came out and said he didn't give her the money. She was higher than a kite, and I believed she had the money in her underwear. I said, "If you don't give me my money," then reached in my pocket and opened a knife, but I didn't pull it out.

She said, "I swear to God, John," and had the audacity to start crying.

I said, "I know how to cry too. If you don't give me my money, Gwen, I'll stick this knife in you right now."

She said, "Please don't kill me, John Lee."

I was shaking because I was getting ready to harm her, but I also knew if I killed her, I was going to be caught. It was broad daylight, and people were out on the corner and their front porches. By the grace of God, I shook my finger at her and said, "Payback. I'll see you," then left.

Fast-forward to the rehearsal room at Soledad, and there's Gene, the saxophone player I stole the diamond watch from a long time ago in San Francisco. My heart started beating really fast. I thought, "Somebody is going to get killed, and it's not going to be me." But then I thought, "It could be me." I looked at Gene with curiosity. Did he recognize me? What is he thinking? Mixed feelings ran through my head: "Is he pretending to not recognize me? I wonder if this guy's setting me up? Maybe he'll get a knife and try to kill me."

Ten months went by, and I realized how doped out I was when I stole the watch. Now I was healthy, my hair had grown out—neat, in an afro— and I had put on weight, going to the gym all the time. By the grace of God, I realized he didn't recognize me.

At Soledad I began to do music shows and was also the prison-yard preacher; I had Bible studies on the lawn. I was blessed to be able to teach a group of guys—Whites, Blacks, and Mexicans. It was a beautiful feeling. I wrote home; word got out, and family and friends began to say, "Junior has changed."

Julie visited me in Soledad while pregnant with our son, Jeremiah; he was born while I was there. When he was one month old, Julie brought him to see me. After Jeremiah grew to be a little boy, his grandma brought him to visit me in San Quentin. It was painful for me to see him in prison: it revealed to me my quality of life and showed me that I was a loser, a thug, and a con player. After visiting time was over, he would ask, "Dad, when are you coming home? I miss you." I knew it would stay in my consciousness for a week or even a month. At night I cried silently under my blanket at my failures, especially my abandonment of my son. I asked God to please help me. On the outside I had to appear to be strong, but on the inside, I wasn't. When inmates cried out loud late at night for whatever reason, they were told, "Shut the f— up, and go to sleep."

While in Soledad I exchanged letters with a convict in Tracy named Bobby Flowers, who was also converted. He suggested that when I got out, I go to a church in West Oakland and study under Pastor Chapman. He said, "He's looking for a young minister, and you going to fit right in there."

Once I got out, I went there; Pastor Chapman could tell I knew the Bible and could expound on certain scriptures. He had a small church, but I needed someone to teach me. I needed to be fed the word of God. Someone recommended I go over to East Oakland to Reverend Doctor W. L. Keeton.

After I was released, I got a job at Giant Foods on East Eighteenth Street in Oakland; I was a security guard in the drug store. Four of my crooked friends heard that I was working there, and believing I was playing a con game, they walked into the store. I saw them from the lookout on the second floor—this store had no security cameras. I ran downstairs; they were going to rampage the place. I told them, "This ain't no game. It ain't like you think. I have accepted Jesus Christ as my personal savior. I have to take care of my family. If I allow you to do this, I don't feed my son. I'm going to feed my son. Y'all got to respect this. Don't do this to me."

It looked like a couple of them had stolen some items, but they said, "I think he's serious. You good, boy." And they left the store. I knew they'd stolen something, but at least they hadn't ransacked the place.

My dad always encouraged me, sending me money, but he was traveling a lot and living in San Carlos at the time. My mother believed I had changed and was my champion. In the past my family told me, "Once a junkie, always a junkie. You ain't gonna be nothin'." Sometimes I believed them, but they taught me a lesson. Now I double dared them. I said, "No, I'm not a junkie. I've changed." One day my mom talked to the garbageman as he was coming through her neighborhood, on Seventy-Third Avenue. She said, "My son just got out, and he done gave his life to the Lord. Can he get a job where you're working?" The garbageman told her what I needed to do. I quit the security job after I was hired and started making good money.

Around this time Julie went to my pastor and said, "John won't marry me." Even though I had doubts about her from the beginning and didn't really love her, we got married where we went to church: Wagoner Memorial Church of God. Julie brought her son Gerry, who was from a previous marriage, from Iowa to live with us. I was preaching the gospel. After around a year, Pastor Keeton told me that the Lord had told him to give me a minister's license because I was learning the word of God. Churches were asking for a minister. Every second Sunday of each month, there were announcements. Sometimes a church would request for me to come and preach there on youth day.

Julie was now working for the post office. I saw an ad for an apartment-manager job near Sobrante Park in Oakland and applied. On the application I wrote under qualifications that I was a trusty at San Quentin State Prison and had managed a tier of inmates who were killers and robbers. I said that I'd run a pretty good tier. The guy called me and gave me the job. When I asked him why he hired me, he said, "Because you were bold enough to tell me your experience. I appreciate that. If you can manage people with those types of mentalities, this will be nothing."

I lived rent free in a remodeled apartment in the building. Julie, Gerry, Jeremiah, and I moved into a place where there weren't as many gunshots every night or crack dealers on every corner, like it had been at our other apartment, on Lockwood in East Oakland. I received my minister's license from Pastor Keeton. I loved what I was doing; I was now going into jails as a chaplain, even to the North County gang unit. Some of the gang members, like Shaka and Rip Saw, knew me from Santa Rita and said, "Wow, man, look at you." I would testify and tell them I had my own apartment and a job, that I was married—it was a beautiful thing. They were amazed someone from the streets could change.

I also became a chaplain in San Quentin, visiting East Block's death row. They don't allow chaplain visits there anymore, but my cousin Pastor Featherstone and I went in; it was unreal. Some were condemned to die, and others would spend the rest of their lives in prison. At each cell I went past, I said, "Good afternoon. How are you? I'm Chaplain John Lee, and I want to know if we can talk today." They didn't want to talk; they cut off all pleasantries. They knew why I was there. One was Muslim. One said he didn't believe in God. I believe most guys on death row don't want to hear about God. They think, "I prayed to God already, and I'm still in the same position," or "I've been talking to him, and he still hasn't answered me. I'm still locked up. I still ain't got my appeal." They want a "microwave God" to get them out of there right away. God will forgive anything, but you have to serve your time. The scriptures say, when talking about paying taxes, "So give back to Caesar what is Caesar's, and to God what is God's" (Matthew: 22:21). You have to pay the consequences.

I recognized one of the Falcon Boys who was doing time for murder in San Quentin; he had grown a little beard and accepted the Muslim faith, but he wasn't really practicing Islam. I said I was from East Oakland as well. As soon as I said that, he came closer to the bars and asked, "Man, can you get me a pen?"

I said, "No, brother, I ain't got no pen." I didn't go so far as to say, "What you going to do with a pen?" I realized that giving a pen to someone sentenced to death could make me an accessory to attempted escape. I had been in the inmate position before; I knew how much time that would carry. It just wasn't right to help give this guy a pen so he could pick the lock, stick the guard in the eye, or try to hurt or kill somebody.

He said, "Right on, right on," and kept staring at me. I told my cousin, who said, "Yeah, they'll ask you for anything. You did the right thing. Just walk away." So that was that.

Things were going great. I bought Julie a car and myself a truck. I started my own business—Brother John's Tree Service. First, I hired a young guy named Peeto from down the street. We dropped fliers in Walnut Creek, Pleasanton, and San Ramon along my garbage route. My business was doing well, and the phone was ringing. Eventually, I had three guys working for me. I was making good money and saving almost every dime. God is faithful, as Paul said: "But my God shall provide all of your need according to his Riches in Christ Jesus" (Philippians 4:19).

# 16

# MY FIRST FALL

Four or five years later, around 1992, my life was going great. I was preaching and doing jail and prison ministry. I had my tree service. I was managing the apartment building and working as a garbageman. I had my wife and two little boys. My life was "Hallelujah!" And I wasn't performing blues. A promoter for one of the biggest blues festivals in California, the Monterey Bay Blues Festival, offered me $3,000 for a forty-minute set; I accepted. A voice in my head told me to grab the fame, the big lights, the money, and especially the beautiful women before they all blew away. When the devil showed Jesus the kingdoms of the world and all their glory, he said, "All this I will give you . . . if you will bow down and worship me" (Matthew 4:9). I bowed down and worshipped the devil instead of saying, like Jesus, "Away from me, Satan! For it is written: 'Worship the Lord your God, and serve Him only'" (Matthew 4:10).

Promotion for the festival was outstanding, with photos of artists in the lineup on posters, on TV, and in most publications. When I took the offer, I didn't think anyone in the church would read the entertainment section; I was dead wrong. After a service Mother Chatmon showed me a newspaper with an ad for the festival and asked, "Is this you?"

There was a photo of me, and I melted; I was so ashamed. "Yes, that's me." I felt like a hypocrite. I preached against the pleasures of the world, but here I was, indulging. The scriptures say, "No one can serve two masters. Either you will hate the one and love the other, or you will be devoted to the one and despise the other" (Matthew 6:24).

The Monterrey Bay Blues festival led to other gigs; I got offers from some of the same clubs my dad played in San Francisco, Palo Alto, and Santa Cruz. It got so bad that when I did a show in San Francisco, I'd have my church clothes ready to change into the next morning. Flash and bling on Saturday, then a suit, tie, and white shirt on Sunday. My late pastor, Dr. L. W. Keeton, yelled at me: "Elder Hooker, you're no entertainer, you're a preacher!" But I felt strong; I thought I could do these things and never pick up spike or pipe for the rest of my life. The scriptures say, "So, if you think you are standing firm, be careful that you don't fall" (1 Corinthians 10:12).

One day, after church services, I went down to Eighty-Third Avenue in East Oakland to check on my sister Shyvonne, like I'd been doing for months—at least that was my excuse. After a few pleasantries, I suddenly said, "Get me two twenty rocks," then handed her two twenty-dollar bills.

She looked at me and said, "Junior, what?"

I said, "Yeah."

She didn't ask again and headed over to a guy standing thirty yards away. She then took me to the crack house. Inside there were four dope fiends sitting around a table, looking for another hit to "take them there" again. I recognized two of them. They looked at me with disbelief; I was sitting at the table with a beautiful suit, hat, and tie, getting ready to get high off crack. I felt a little uncomfortable, dumb, and stupid—a little like the marks I'd burned. My sister loaded the pipe, took the first hit, and passed it to me. I hit it, and my head went to the ceiling; it felt like I was in a different orbit. *Boom!* I was back in the same vomit that had sent me back and forth to prisons.

I was leading a double life—playing blues gigs and preaching in church. I had three jobs: apartment management, garbage collection, and my tree service, which I mostly worked on the weekends. After the garbage collection job ended around twelve or one o'clock in the afternoon, I'd swing by the day care to pick up Jeremiah. I was raising two boys with a wife who was difficult. Julie didn't communicate with me or help me out with the business, even to write checks. She cursed around the boys. Things were tense between us. One day she got angry and called me the N-word. Another time she called the police on me for no reason, or rather it was to have me put out of the apartment in Oakland. When they arrived, I had my marriage license in my back pocket to prove that I belonged there.

When they saw the license, one officer said, "We can't just put him out. This is a civil matter." After the police left, she looked at me, shaking her head, and said, "Who carries their marriage license in their back pocket?"

My life had become unmanageable. Pressures in your household should never be used as an excuse for destroying your life, but I was weak and succumbed. There's always a spot in the back of a drug addict's mind: either you're in denial, or you fool yourself into believing you'll do it just the one time. I just needed to relieve the pressure, but it doesn't work like that.

Looking back, I think my seed of faith first fell among the thorns. The scriptures say the devil can get ahold of a person because of the cares of the world. The temptation of money, cocaine, overwhelming attention, women slipping me their phone numbers—it was all too much. It loosened the anchor of my faith: "There is nothing concealed that will not be disclosed, or hidden that will not be made known. What you have said in the dark will be heard in the daylight, and what you have whispered in the ear in the inner rooms will be proclaimed from the roofs" (Luke 12:2-3). My deceit came to light. The Lord didn't want it to happen, but he allowed it. He could have stopped it, but he saw that the life I'm living now would come.

Julie took the boys on vacation to visit her mother and father in Iowa. I tried to keep my secret, but to no avail. Julie didn't know it when she left, but Pastor Keeton knew something was wrong. I missed church every Sunday; I wasn't answering phone calls, because I was hooked again. Finally, Pastor Keeton and the late Deacon Chapmon came by the apartment and called to me, "Elder Hooker, we know you're in there, son. Come out and let's talk. Let us pray for you."

I wouldn't open the door; I cried until they walked back down the stairs. My wife would later learn how I was back in my sins. Understandably, she didn't want the boys around dope and my criminal behavior, so she eventually left and moved to Vallejo. I wanted badly to be around my family. No matter what kind of dope-fiend dog you are, there's a soft spot for family. I missed playing with those boys. I didn't like walking the streets, being in jail cells, or sleeping in the back of my truck: that's what a life of drugs is. It makes you think about the fun times you've had with your family. So I asked Julie if I could come back; she made me promise to kick the habit. I swore to God I would quit, and she allowed me to move to Vallejo. I gave up the apartment manager job to be with her and the boys. She had moved into an apartment without any furniture just to get away from me. I had the furniture shipped to the new apartment and asked for two weeks' leave of absence from my garbage collection job, and the company approved. There were rumors around the company I was using dope. I came to find out that they did know. People had driven past a dope stroll and seen me, plus my behavior of showing up late was noticeable.

I kicked the habit cold turkey. I laid in bed with cold chills and sweats—I'm talking about shaking chills like it's 20 below in Detroit, Michigan, and sweats like it's 130 degrees outside in Arizona. My bones ached; I lost weight. I couldn't walk, because my ankles felt like they had arthritis. I had diarrhea. My eyes were watering, then burning. I was delirious. If I did fall asleep, I had nightmares that quickly woke me up. I was tossing and turning. I got the nastiest tastes in my mouth; I hate to say it, but saliva would build up, and I was constantly spitting and going to the toilet. I was throwing up, and then all of a sudden, my mouth would turn dry, like I was in a desert. I felt like I just couldn't do it, but I hung in there. With each day that passed, I got better.

During that time, one thing Julie asked me to do was pick up Jeremiah. I would get up, walk over to the bus stop, and walk Jeremiah back to the house, fixing him a sandwich or cereal—he loved cereal. Then I'd go and lay back down.

After two weeks I went back to work. Someone at work said, "Look, John, I need to talk to you. I kind of know what's going on with you, man. That's why we allowed you to take them two weeks. We're here for you. We want you to know you're not the only one that's gone through something like this. It happens all the time. Some with alcoholism, some with other issues, so we got you. Just do the right thing."

I stayed clean about a week or two; it didn't take long, and my addiction was back. Like a werewolf at a full moon, I was howling for dope. One day, when I was sleeping through one of my drug stupors, someone tapped my shoulder and said, "Mr. Hooker, it's time to go."

Julie had called the sheriff's office; he was serving papers for a divorce and an order to vacate the property. I was stunned! Julie said, "It's over, John Lee. Your stuff is right here, in this suitcase. I can't take this no more. It's over."

The sheriff asked if she wanted my pickup truck, and she said, "No, that's all he has." She was right; I had even spent the $25,000 I had saved for my son's college. I was dead broke with nowhere to go.

I went to stay in one of my dad's homes in Vallejo, where his saxophone player, Kenny, also lived. The next day, I overslept and nervously called my job to say I would be in the following day. The supervisor said, "Sorry, John, you've been dismissed. Too many absences and late arrivals." I lay on the couch and thought, "What now?" I was divorced, fired, back on dope, and broke. I thought about suicide, but I didn't have the nerve to face God with charges of murder, hypocrisy, and lying against me. I knew the scripture: thou shalt not murder—even thyself. God created me, so I belong to him.

I was kicked out of the Vallejo home after Kenny was robbed and murdered in East Palo Alto while on his way home from a gig. I couldn't be trusted to remain there alone.

I found out Julie had moved to Richmond and rented a house. While Julie was at work, I would sneak through the window, take a bath, sleep, and raid the refrigerator. When the kids came home from school, they'd wake me up. I was the same old dog; Julie put me out again. One day someone told me, "A White woman just threw some clothes and shoes into your pickup truck." I looked outside and saw my life in the back of the dirty pickup and scattered on the ground. In 1994 Julie took the kids, left North Richmond and me, and moved back to Iowa.

I slept in the backseat of my truck and washed up at gas stations or snuck into hotel bathrooms. I shortchanged retailers: snatch, grab, and run. I ate in grocery markets, walking down the aisles and eating Vienna sausages, salami, cheese, soda crackers, or bread. I had turned into a vagrant.

In North Richmond I went back to playing the con game. One night I broke a young dope dealer who was about fourteen years old by shaking the red card. He bet $200; when he turned the black card over, his eyes got real wide. I scooped the money up, and he demanded it back: "Dude, you cheated me." He pulled out a pistol, and I started running, but he got me, shooting me in my left ankle. I ran to the dope house with a pocketful of money, ordered cocaine, and smoked it. After two or three hours, I left, took a cab to BART, and went to Oakland. I got off at the Coliseum and went to Shyvonne's house.

Shyvonne asked me what happened; I told her I'd gotten shot. Then I told her to go get us sixty dollars' worth of crack. She didn't ask, "Should

I call an ambulance?" That's what dope fiends do: get high first, call the ambulance later. When she came back, we smoked. I finally went to the corner of East Fourteenth Street and called 911 from a phone booth. At Highland Hospital they didn't remove the bullet; they just sewed me up. The bullet wasn't taken out until after three more prison terms, when I went back to Sierra Jamestown Conservation Camp.

After being homeless and sleeping at dope houses, sleezy hotels, and abandoned houses, I was sent back to San Quentin, to the reception center in West Block—where once I had acted as minister of the gospel. It was God's way of telling me, "You reap what you sow." I came and went so many times from San Quentin, it was like a second home. The sergeant would call my name first to prove he was right when he'd said, "You'll be back, Hooker."

I would say with a smile, "Don't hold your breath, Sarge."

San Quentin was a filthy joint full of pigeons, seagulls, undercover child molesters, killers, thieves, racists, and gang members. You always had to keep an eye out, even when you were laughing at some old street stories. If there was a wire out on the prison grapevine that you had to watch your back, you would be sure to wear your boots to the shower. The saying "Don't get caught with your boots off" is as true in prison as it is for adultery: you'd better be ready. I had a job in the dry-cleaning department and stayed pressed; I was what the convicts called "penitentiary sharp." When prisoners wanted their clothes pressed to look good for a visit, a photo shoot on the yard, or an introduction to someone from the street, they paid me with goods from the canteen. My locker was full of what we called zoom-zooms and wham-whams (sweet junk food). Kim Turner worked in the officer's mess hall and had access to the best foods; when he cooked, he would steal their food and bring it out for us to have a spread. Sonny Hill worked in the upper yard of the kitchen and stole coffee and Kool-Aid. I made sure their clothes looked good. We often laugh today about how we used to be.

When I got out of San Quentin, I headed to the Tenderloin in San Francisco to hustle. Most of the drug addicts and homeless folks there were like zombies. If you didn't have a hustle, you begged, borrowed, or robbed.

One day, when I was walking through the 'hood wearing a brand-new black jacket, a dope-dealing youngster said, "Hey, that's my jacket." Five kids jumped me; I fought back. As I was trying to get up, one of them kicked all my front teeth out. I later used the missing teeth to my advantage when tricking people out of their money: I looked more like an African needing help.

Another time I stopped a White guy who was coming across Market Street in San Francisco. When he asked if I needed anything, I went into my drag voice and tricked him out of a sack of dope. Then he told his boss, who followed me into a liquor store. We began arguing and fighting inside the store. I tripped over a case of beer; he jumped on top of me and pressed a knife into my face. He cut me, but I wrestled him off, and he ran away. I heard the storeowner say, "Hey, man, stop it. Get out of here, or I will call the police." My face was bleeding; I wear the scar today as a reminder of the days when God kept me away from death.

A year later, at Avenal Prison, I ran into that guy who'd cut my face. I was in the yard, hitting the heavy bag, as he was getting off the bus. He looked over at me from about fifty yards away; I hit the bag a little harder. The next day, he came looking for me and watched me hit the bag with a passive smile on his face. I told him, "You know what, man? What goes around, comes around. We both was in the mix in them streets. I know I was wrong. I took your dope. We're going to let bygones be bygones. I ain't going to do nothing to you, and you ain't got to watch your back."

Every day he saw me, he smiled and asked, "How you doing, Magic?" With all the wrong that I've done, I have to forgive people.

# 17

# MY BAND IN REDWOOD CITY AND SECOND MARRIAGE

I was released from San Quentin in 1998. That was the last time: I never again went back to prison as a convicted felon. Later, by the power and grace of God, I returned as a prison chaplain. My dad had moved to Hastings Street in Redwood City and kindly invited me to come live with him. He even picked me up in a limousine at the bus station, saying, "Get in, boy. You probably ain't never been in a limo fo', have you? Sit down." He was always a show-off in a humorous way. I laughed.

He said, "So good to see you. You look good, Junior." Seeing my missing teeth, he asked, "Did that gang in San Francisco hurt you?"

"Nah, I'm okay."

He said, "Well, I got a good dentist." My dad paid for me to get my teeth fixed. I was so embarrassed by those missing teeth that I'd been afraid to laugh or talk.

We then had a father-to-son talk about that stuff I didn't really want to talk about. He said, "One day, I got to leave this earth. You got a great voice. You a great entertainer. You're not like anybody else. You know how to tell stories, just like I do. But you tell your parts of the story. Be you and nobody else. The world already has a John Lee Hooker and a B. B. King. They don't need another one. Junior, you're original."

I didn't want to hear it, but he said, "One day, after I'm gone, this house here in Redwood City is going be yours. Your sister got one, your other sister got one, your brother got one, and you got the last one. Start your own band, travel the world, and the good Lawd gonna bless you."

He called John Garcia, his guitar player, and told him I was home and forming a band. John never asked for a dime. We got a band together, rehearsed, and recorded three songs. Now that I was clean and sober, I changed my dad's famous song "One Bourbon, One Scotch, and One Beer" to "One Coke, One Sprite, and Root Beer."

Sometimes I opened for my dad, introducing him with "Now, ladies and gentlemen, are you ready for the Boogie Man? My father and your father of the blues, the king of the boogie himself, John Lee Hooker." All the time, he was smiling, listening, and watching so happily. He would laugh and say, "Stop it, boy."

When he was ready to close the show, he would bring me back out onstage to do a boogie together. Everybody stood up. After a few bars, he'd raise his hand, wave, and walk off. The crowd loved my dad. What a showman!

My dad bought me a truck to start another tree service. I took the truck in one day to be checked at a Kia dealer; when I went to pick it up, a woman named Brenda told the lady who'd been initially helping me that she would take care of me. She asked to see my ID, then said, "John Lee Hooker Jr. Really?" In my mind I was thinking, "Here we go." We talked and she asked about my next gig. I told her we were going to be in the Boom Boom Room in San Francisco.[1] She told me she had never been to a blues concert and wanted to go. She asked me if she could attend and gave me her number. When I went to give her my phone number, she said, "Oh, I already have your number and address on the receipt."

She was a pretty lady, twenty years younger than me, and had a son. She called a few times, and I invited her to the house before the gig. My dad said, "Ooh wee, that girl pretty, boy. Where you meet her at?" And he asked her, "Where's your mom at? What do your mama look like? I bet you took after your mama." Nobody had ever talked to Brenda like that.

After we got back from the gig, nighttime came, and it was time for her to go home, but she asked if she could get cleaned up. I knew instantly what that meant: she came into my room with a negligee on. She'd had this planned the whole time, assuming I would say yes to her spending the night. She wanted to have sex, but I was reluctant. I was thinking about San Quentin.

At San Quentin they had the prisoners with HIV segregated in the gym, away from the general population, for fear of the disease spreading by sexual contact. They checked everyone who came into the prison on a regular basis. After they drew your blood, you went back to your cell and waited three, four, or even five days, and if they called you in the middle of the day and said, "Roll 'em up. You're being transferred to the gym," that meant you had HIV. When they told me I was clean, I couldn't believe it. I was so reckless with women and drug paraphernalia. I was so desperate that I'd shot dope without thoroughly cleaning it out. One time I went to Red Dave's tent when he wasn't there. I was so sick; my nose was running, my skin sweating, and my bones hurting, and I was about to go to the bathroom on myself. I bought the dope but didn't have an outfit, so I dug around inside his makeshift tent, found a syringe, and didn't even rinse it out. I had to rush and shoot the dope to feel better.

I was so sick another time that I went to Bugs's house. He wasn't there, but other people were, including a White guy—a big-time dope dealer—sitting there with a needle in his arm. I asked for Bugs, and he told me Bugs had gone on a run. I said, "I'm sick as a dog. I need to borrow some dope on credit."

He said, "Man, I know how that feels. I ain't got nothing, but I can't finish all this. It's too much for me." He slid me the cooker, pulled the needle out of his arm, and squirted the dope back with his blood in it. I was so sick, I shot the dope with his blood. That dope was so good, it was screaming—I mean, awfully good. I got well and high at the same time. That's how desperate I was, and that's how coldhearted I was to my own self. I had no self-esteem: my attitude was "I ain't dead yet. I won't die. I can't die." I was an absolute fool.

While I was in San Quentin getting tested, I thought about all those episodes. I saw guys being told they had HIV. They were so ashamed; they were told they should get ready to die. I thought about HIV that night with Brenda. When she wanted to get romantic, I said, "You got any protection?"

She said, "No."

I said, "I'm sorry, but we'll have to wait."

As bad as I wanted to sleep with her, I didn't do it. It reminded me of how many dangerous chances I had taken while not in my right mind. But this time, by the grace of God, I didn't take a chance. I believed her when she said she was clean, but I had to be sure. I told her, "I promised myself and the world I'm not doing nothing unless I know 100 percent I won't get infected. I hope you understand."

The next morning, she probably thought, "What kind of dude is this? He's just gotten out of prison and doesn't want to make love?" A smart dude. Today I thank God that in my seventies, I'm free of disease and don't take any medication.

During this time I started up another tree service and landscape business. Brenda worked as a secretary at the Kia dealership. On weekends I drove from Redwood City to Oakland to go to church with Pastor Keeton. As time passed I am ashamed to say I fell again. The Bible says, "For though the righteous fall seven times, they rise again" (Proverbs 24:16). Big Mama, my dad, and my mom all taught me to work for what's mine, not to give up. They taught me to fight back. "You fight, you get whupped. Just fight back. Don't stop fighting." I failed, I got back up, and I fell again.

After about eight months, Brenda moved in. One day she said, "Do you know what I want you to do? Ask me to be your wife." I found it funny because no one had ever said that to me. We got married at my dad's big house. By then he had moved to Los Altos. But I was so loaded, my sister Diane had to guide me around so I didn't fall or burn the house to the ground with my cigarettes.

On the way home from the wedding, Brenda and I got into an argument. I asked Brenda, "Who the hell do you think I am? A fool? Who marries a drug addict? Who?"

She was trying to make it look like it was a good thing she was with me. I said, "No, it's not. If you recall, *you* said you wanted me to propose to you. But who marries a dope fiend without some ulterior motive? This marriage won't last a year. You watch."

She said, "What are you trying to say?"

I said, "Who do you think you're talking to? I've been in the streets, in prison. I've been doing this life since before you was born. I saw you coming. There is a wall of protection all the way around me, legally and spiritually. There's no way you can touch me."

She said, "I'm your wife."

She was probably a gold digger who wanted financial security. Maybe she wanted notoriety or experience from someone who was older, but she was also fascinated with celebrity and the mystique of being around glamor. She'd watch me onstage and brag to her girlfriends. She thought she could meet some famous people at my dad's house, and she did: tailors who flew in to fit us for suits, Charlie Musslewhite, Van Morrison, and John Lee Hooker, who called her his pretty daughter.

I was so hooked, I would go to the Tenderloin in San Francisco and not come home for several days. Once Brenda came looking for me at the Henry Hotel, driving my black Cadillac. She knew my nickname was Magic. When she asked for me, some tried to flirt with her. I give her credit: as a young White girl, Brenda was brave. She never did find me in the Tenderloin, but she found me at San Francisco General Hospital when I overdosed. When I called my dad and told him I was in the hospital, he said, "Junior, you going to kill yourself. Your wife is worried to death, looking for you. She's been everywhere. I told her where you are."

When they wheeled me out on a gurney, Brenda was there at the hospital, with a disapproving look. I said, "I really don't want to hear this right now." She was there to take me back to Redwood City.

While we were driving home, I had ten dollars in my pocket. When she stopped at a red light, I bounced out of the car and told her I would see her that night. She cursed and cursed; I walked away, headed to the Tenderloin to shoot some dope.

# 18

# MY FATHER'S DEATH AND MY THIRD AND FINAL FALL

Finally, after I was picked up for driving under the influence twice, a judge sent me to a drug program. Brenda visited me every week, bringing me clothes. When I got out, I had lost my tree service. Some people I knew in Oakland helped me get a great job working construction in South San Francisco for Malcolm Drilling. I'd ride my bike to the bus station, put the bike on the front of the bus, and ride to South San Francisco. One day, on June 21, 2001, it was hot, and I was in the trenches. The foreman came and said, "John Lee, there's a lady up above, calling for you. She said your dad has just died." I dropped what I was doing and ran up the hill; Brenda was up there. I took my shirt and pulled it up over my head and just cried. She drove me to my dad's house in Los Altos.

My mother and family were there. My dad was lying in the bed; he looked peaceful and calm. When I saw him, I cried. I pulled my chair up, the one I always sat in when I visited him. He would say, "Come on in, Preacher Reverend Junior." He used to brag about me: "Here, y'all, that's Reverend Junior. That boy come a long ways. That boy done been in seven prisons. I even played up in one of them prisons. I thought they was going to lock me up. He went to the parow board."

I'd say, "Parole board, Dad."

He would say, "Whatever. I sung him out of there."

Dad always said, "Just do me one favor before I go. Let me see you clean and sober."

When I accepted the Lord in my life, he said, "I can sleep now at night, Junior, knowing you ain't in them streets or in one of them prisons." He was able to see me walk in his home with my clergy clothes on and say, "Hey, Reverend Junior, sit down, boy." My father wasn't religious, but he was happy I was saved. The Lord had delivered me from drugs and alcohol.

I put my head on my dad's cold face and kissed him on the forehead. I put the side of my face on his and held him for a while. Brenda walked up to me and said, "Baby, these were on the floor." She handed me his watch and diamond ring, and I put them in my pocket.

His funeral was attended by the entire family and all his friends; no photos of his deceased body were allowed. It was bittersweet: we were sad he was gone but happy he wasn't in pain anymore. My dad's memorial was held at the Mormon Tabernacle in the Oakland Hills and was open to the public. The city closed Interstate 280 to allow the funeral procession to flow without delays. Legendary musicians, like Buddy Guy and Bonnie Raitt, were in attendance to pay their respects.

My dad was gone, and I was still working. One day Brenda and I got into an argument. She was cursing and walked toward me in an adversarial way. I'd never hit a woman, but I'm a boxer, and my defense mechanism kicked in. When she stretched out her arm toward my face, I grabbed her by the arms. I told her, "Don't walk up on me like you're going to hit me."

She yelled, telling me to let her go, and I did. Then she came toward me again. She said, "I'm not going to let you hit me," and she was crying. She picked up the phone, called the police, and left.

After a while there was a knock at the door. Brenda had the police with her. The police said, "Put your hands behind your back."

I asked, "What is this about?"

"You're under arrest for domestic violence."

They asked Brenda if she was going to stay there that night; she said no, grabbed her son, and they left.

The police took me to jail. I felt so bad, especially after having gone all of that time with no arrests. I was doing well with the tree service, working construction, and going to church every week, sometimes two or three times. I called Zakiya and told her I was in jail. When I told her why, she said, "Junior, you ain't hit that girl." Then she asked me, "Is she still there?" I said I didn't know, because I was in jail. My sister called

Brenda and said, "Let me tell you something. I'm coming over there. You better not be in there. Get your stuff, and get out of his house. You told them police and lied about my brother. We coming out there. You better not be there, b—."

Zakiya got me out on bail. When I got to the house, Brenda was gone. There was a note that said, "I took me and my son out of here. When you get out of jail, do whatever you need to do. But I just couldn't take it." She went somewhere, taking all of her stuff with her.

Stressed out from being locked up, my dad dying, and Brenda leaving, I headed straight to East Oakland, copped some dope, and got high. Soon I was hooked on dope again, going back and forth from Oakland to the Tenderloin. One night on my way home, I was pulled over and arrested for my fourth DUI—I already had a third case pending in Redwood City.

After several months passed, I developed an abscess in my left arm so large that you could stick your finger in it. After I couldn't find any more veins in my arms, I started shooting dope in my neck. I missed the vein and developed a second abscess in my neck. Exhausted and sick, I reluctantly called my mother from San Francisco. She told me to take a taxi to her place in Berkeley. I fell asleep in the taxi on the way there. I had been awake for three days straight.

When I got to Berkeley, I went to the church next door to my mother's house and asked for Mother Hooker. She came out; when she saw the condition I was in, she helped me walk back to her house, told me to take a shower, made a sandwich for me, and gave me one of my niece's big T-shirts and some walking shorts to sleep in. Then she made a place for me to sleep on the floor. Once I had recovered a little, she brought me back to Redwood City, but I told her I owed bills. My finances were a mess; I was about to lose my house to foreclosure because I had fallen behind in my mortgage payments. My mother decided to give up her place and move in with me so she could take financial control and stop the foreclosure.

I didn't stop doing drugs; in fact, the abscess in my neck became infected. Sick and without a vehicle, I asked my mother and sister Karen to drop me off in San Francisco; I said I needed to get some medication for my dope sickness or I would die. I told them I needed to get well, but they knew I was lying. When they pulled up and saw all the drugged-out people standing on the corner, they begged me, "Junior, please don't go." They were worried I would get killed. I told them I would be fine, to trust me. I went in and got high. After getting high, I was standing on a corner with a bunch of drug addicts. And to this day I believe it was God who sent an ambulance just for me. I was wearing a neck brace to hide the ugly swollen abscess. The ambulance attendant got out, walked straight toward me, and asked if he could help me. I said, "What do you mean? I didn't call you."

He said, "Let me help you, young man."

I continued to reject his pleas: "What are you talking about? Ain't nothing wrong with me."

Someone next to me gently prompted me, saying, "Magic, please go with him. Let him help you, man." I relented, and they took me to a hospital in San Francisco. They did an MRI; they said my heart was slow but that I needed surgery to remove the abscess or I could die of infection. A friend of mine was operated on for the same thing and became a paraplegic. Fearing I could die too, I began to cry as my ruined life flashed before me. The doctor said, "Don't worry, you'll be alright." The operation was successful; afterward, I called my sister Diane and told her where I was and what had happened.

Diane visited me in the hospital, but I was drained physically and mentally. My dad was gone, my marriage was over, and I was back on the streets. In addition, I could have died on the operating table. After seven or eight days, I was transferred to a Kaiser hospital in Redwood City. After I recovered, my sister Shyvonne brought me home, and my mother nursed me back to health. She took care of me, cooked, washed cloths, sang spiritual hymns, and prayed for me. Once I was a little better, she asked me where my jewelry and clothes were. I told her my clothes were at the cleaners and that I'd pawned all my jewelry. We went to the pawn shop together to get back a Longines watch and two diamond rings I had pawned for $350—they were worth several thousand. As we were leaving the pawn shop, I saw two hustlers I used to hang out with getting ready to hit a lick. Seeing me with my mother, they said, "This ain't you, man. Don't come back down here, Magic."

I told them, "I'm through with this."

At the cleaners, picking up my clothes, we saw some con players, who just waved goodbye. They could see I had changed.

After all I had been through physically and mentally, I asked God to forgive me and prevent me from ever using drugs again. I had nearly died so many times. One time, in my father's basement, I overdosed behind the bar. My dad and his personal manager heard the crash of beer bottles from upstairs as I hit the ground. They came running down and called an ambulance. I was rushed to Highland Hospital. I remember waking and seeing my body coming up, just bouncing off the table—*boom*—because they applied paddles to restart my heart.

I had finally had enough. I felt I was at my rock bottom. I was finally through with the streets. A giant relief came over me: God had forgiven me and delivered me from the desire for the devil's dope.

For my family, my drug addiction caused heartaches, sleepless nights, tears, fussing, and fighting. They kicked me out, threatened to shoot me, and threw skillets at me. Sometimes I would think about my uncle and my family telling me, "Once a dope fiend, always a dope fiend." I had failed three times; the devil was telling me it wouldn't work—Jesus wouldn't work. But I kept on fighting and kept on praying. I don't want anyone to think it was due to my strength, but I had a will to be clean and sober. In the past if someone told me they'd gotten clean and sober after twenty years with the help of God, I couldn't grasp that mentally. But I knew deep down inside that it was true for me, because I'd asked God, "If you can do it for them, you can do it for me," and he did.

After I was clean and sober, there was still the problem of my fourth DUI: this one was in San Francisco, and I had a third pending in Redwood City. A public defender from San Francisco called me and said, "You're supposed to be in court over here in San Francisco on the same day you need to appear in Redwood City. If the judge in Redwood City learns you got another DUI here, you'll do four years in prison. That's the law. I'm going to enter a guilty plea in absentia for this one, but I'll do it later. You go to court in Redwood City first, and enter your guilty plea. They have evidence against you."

My mother took me to court; I thought I would not be coming back. I didn't want my mother to be there and pleaded with her, but she came in anyway. When they called my name, I saw her put her head down, praying in the courtroom. I told her before we went in, "Prayer's not going to help me."

The judge called my case, read my charges, looked up at me, and said, "You've got three DUIs, young man. Do you know I can send you away from here? What am I going to do with you, Mr. Hooker? I'm not going to send you away. I believe you are salvageable. I'm going to send you to a drug program for six months and suspend your sentence."

I looked over at my mother, who had her right hand in the air and was looking up to heaven. She appeared to be mouthing, "Thank you, Jesus." I knew God had heard her, because now I am saved, sanctified, and filled with the Holy Ghost—clean and sober.

They told me I had thirty days to find a drug program. In 2003 I entered Moriah House for six months. I asked my mother not to come visit, as I couldn't have visits for the first three months. It was a twelve-step program with meetings. After three or four months, I noticed something about the director, Grant Davis. He would go out, stay out late, and come back loaded—scratching and nodding in front of the computer. I called "Fast Eddie" Vandervoort, the owner of Moriah House, and said, "Look, Eddie, this is John Lee. I am gathering all ten of us, and we're going back to the Redwood City courtroom to tell the judge we need to be in another program. Your director is at the computer, nodding off on heroin while all of us are trying to get clean. This is too tempting for the weaker people. We're out of here."

He said, "Please, don't go, John. Don't do this to me. What can I do? Why don't you take over as director? You're a leader. They love you there. What about it, Johnny? How much, man?"

I said, "Eddie, this is what I want: a salary of $1,500 every two weeks and the opportunity to go to church and visit my family every week. I want to be able to do my music wherever it calls me." Without any hesitation, he gave me everything I asked for. This was unbelievable. He fired the director and made me the new sheriff in town.

I had been to drug programs in San Francisco, Oakland, Palo Alto, San Jose, and Santa Clara, as well as to a cult in Los Angeles and Oakland. I went to prisons, and still, I would get out and fall flat on my face—up until the time I found the Lord Jesus Christ (or he found me)—because I was the one who was lost. In Moriah House I didn't fully embrace him, because I was still singing music about this world; something still wasn't right. But I never used drugs again after I entered that program.

# 5

# FROM THE BLUES TO
# THE GOOD NEWS

FROM THE BLUES TO
THE GOOD NEWS

# 19

# MUSICAL SUCCESS

While I was at my new job as the director at Moriah House, I got a band together with the help of the late Cynthia Handy: her brother John Handy was on drums; then there was Big Craig Robinson on bass, Will "Roc" Griffin on keyboard, and Jeffrey James Horan and John Garcia on guitar. John was a music teacher, so he couldn't always accept work on the road. At the age of sixteen, Jeffrey James went on tour with us.

I had enough money put away to buy a van and have it delivered to the front door of the drug program, with the permission of the owner. As a stipulation of my probation, I had to have breathalyzers installed in any vehicle I owned and also had to take driver's education classes. Thanks be to God, I never touched heroin, alcohol, or cigarettes again.

We rehearsed at different places. I used the computer at Moriah House to book my own gigs. The first gig was in downtown Redwood City. We also played the Catalyst in Santa Cruz and various other cool places in the Bay Area. While I was still in the drug program, they even allowed me to hit the road for two or three weeks to go out to Lyons, Colorado; Salt Lake City; Las Vegas; Seattle; and New Mexico. I was so happy to be working without the crutch of drugs.

We got to Lyons a week and a half too early, but that was fine—we were so happy to be out on the road, and I was happy not to be listening to the devil's voice to go find dope. The promoter, Dave McIntire, put us up and gave us food until we moved to a hotel: Jeffrey James Horan, John Handy, and I shared one room, and Craig and Will slept in the van until the date of the gig. The gig started, and we tore the place up. It was sold out, so they asked for one more night. After that we hit the road, traveling to different gigs.

I finished my time in Moriah House, and when I wasn't on the road, I lived in the house in Redwood City that my dad had given me. We toured all over the United States. Will "Roc," my band director and keyboard player, contacted Morey Alexander, the president at Kent Records, and told him he needed to record John Lee Hooker Jr. I was writing my own songs with the creative help of the instrumentalists backing me. We recorded *Blues with a Vengeance*. Because we were doing so well, Will said, "You're going to need management." Stuart Woltz at Kent recommended Ron Kramer. I met with Ron and his partner, Brian Panella. Ron explained his percentage, and I agreed. He'd helped sign Johnny "Guitar" Watson to DJM Records and had worked for EMI/Capitol Records; he knew the music game inside and out.

*Blues with a Vengeance* was released in 2004 and did well. We came out with our own style of music, not an impression of my dad, B. B. King, or anyone else. One day, while I was packing to go on our first European tour, I got a phone call from Stuart Woltz, and it sounded like he was crying. He said, "Junior, you've just been nominated for a Grammy." I said, "No way." I had just gotten out of San Quentin not too long ago. But it was true: *Blues with a Vengeance* was nominated in 2004 for Best Traditional Blues Album, along with Etta James (who won), Eric Clapton, B. B. King, and Pinetop Perkins. Stuart told me how proud he was of me: "I watched you make those steps. I saw you delivered from the use of dope." A day or two after the Grammy nomination, the album was nominated for the W. C. Handy Debut Artist Award from the Blues Foundation, which I won. Those two nominations opened a lot of doors for me.

At the Grammy Awards ceremony at the Staples Center, I met the great gospel singer and pastor Shirley Caesar. When I saw her, I stopped in my tracks. She asked me who I was. When I told her I was John Lee Hooker Jr., she started making the bow-down sign to me. I said, "No, no," and starting bowing down to her. "You're the star, not me."

Shirley Caesar had been a great motivation to me; I'd listened to her music in San Quentin, Avenal, and Soledad prisons on gospel radio and the CD players guys had on the yard. I really appreciated her storytelling, like in "Hold My Mule (Shoutin' John)." In that song, Shoutin' John attends a "dead church" and keeps shouting for joy. The usher gets upset with him for being disruptive and warns him to stop his loud behavior. The clergy go out to his house and say, "If you don't stop shoutin' / If you don't stop dancin' / We gon' put you outta our church."[1] Shoutin' John tells them he's received blessings from God: he's healthy, his children are not in prison or on drugs, and he starts praising the Lord right there. Then they understand why he behaves the way he does. In her song "Satan, You're a Liar," she tells a story I can relate to: Talking directly to the devil, she tells him he said she "would never make it" and "wouldn't last." Then she calls him a liar because she is saved.[2] What a great moment for me to meet someone whose music meant so much to me! She was an inspiration.

After my dad's death, his house went up for sale in Los Altos; it was a big place with five bedrooms, a smaller cottage on the property, a Jacuzzi, and a swimming pool. I would go over and mow the lawn and check all the rooms, making sure the place was immaculate. This was a daily routine I had for about two months; it became a habit. I was awakened out of it by a phone call from my sister Zakiya. She said, "Junior, you still mourning dad. You got to let it go, brother. The only way you're going to break that cycle is to move out of Redwood City, or you going to just keep floating with the memories of Daddy. Let him journey. He's gone, Junior."

My sister helped me snap out of it. She was right: the house in Redwood City that I was living in reminded me of my dad. I remember my dad saying that when he moved to different cities or flipped houses, he always made sure he was near an airport, a supermarket, a bank, and that the house was on a cul-de-sac with privacy and security. While playing a gig in Sacramento, I met a real estate agent named Dodie; she helped me find a beautiful home in Roseville, in the Sacramento area, with all the things my dad recommended.

I toured the United States, Canada (Ottawa, Montreal, Vancouver), and Europe. I performed at the Thunder Bay Blues Festival in Ontario, Canada, in July 2004; it was explosively jubilant. In September I played the San Francisco Blues Festival at Fort Mason. That was really exciting; the place was packed. I remember going to Charlie Musselwhite's dressing room. It was the first time Charlie and I had seen each other since the 1970s, when my dad was alive; now we were both clean and sober. We hugged and Charlie said, "I miss your dad, Junior."

I told him, "Yeah, I do too." We laughed at some stories about my dad and the jokes he would tell. That was a great highlight to me.

That year, I played Biscuits and Blues, a club in San Francisco. My friends Tina and Steve Suen always booked me to play a show there on New Year's Eve. We toured, playing big festivals and small clubs. I was getting invitations from all over the world—it was a whirlwind. One day I was driving in my van with Kim Turner when the phone rang. It was a promoter named Peter Noble; he was calling from Australia to book me in Perth and Melbourne and for the Bluesfest in Byron Bay. He offered me $30,000 to play for one week. I pulled over and double-parked. Kim kept talking to me. I told him, "Man, be quiet. This is important. This is Australia on the phone."

In Australia we opened for George Clinton and Parliament Funkadelic, and Dave Matthews. It was a big bill. I was so jetlagged—we had just performed in Spain and Germany before flying to Australia. In Europe we'd played theaters and opera houses—top-of-the-line venues. We stayed on the road for a month.

Being on the road and touring while clean and sober was a new experience and a blessed one. I knew people were just being kind when they offered marijuana, a drink, or a sniff of cocaine; one guy even offered me heroin. And it felt so wonderful to be in control of my life and tell someone, "No thanks, I don't do drugs." The apostle Paul said, "For we know that our old self was crucified with him so that the body ruled by sin might be done away with, that we should no longer be slaves to sin—because anyone who has died has been set free from sin" (Romans 6:6–7). I didn't go to after-parties or late-night jam sessions. Satan tested Jesus, leading him to the highest point of the temple and saying, "'If you are the Son of God, . . . throw yourself down from here.' . . . Jesus answered, 'It is said: "Do not put the Lord your God to the test"'" (Luke 4:9–12). I didn't tempt God; I didn't go places thinking I was Superman or could take it. I just didn't go. It's after the fact that you feel like a piece of garbage; giving into temptation doesn't feel good. When I said no, I felt victory.

It felt so good to be on stage singing, performing, and making people smile; I didn't need the booster shot of dope. Everything was natural. I didn't feel like I was plugged into an extension cord providing the fake energy I needed to hit another note or to dance. During the downtime on the road, I always found a fitness center in the hotel or around town. I would even do calisthenics in my room. I prayed, called people, and wrote songs; I was never bored. One time I received an invitation through my website to go to an AA meeting in Durango, Colorado. People came up to me afterward and gave me a chip as a souvenir—it was really special. In Europe the doors to all the churches are always open, so I went in, kneeled, and prayed.

But deep down inside, I felt I was in the wrong work places: clubs and venues that sold hard liquor and even drugs and sex. I asked the Lord for strength and thanked him for each and every day. You need strength on the road. It's a jungle—drug demons can easily attack through the guise of a woman or a kind man—but I stayed strong.

My next album, *Cold as Ice*, was released in 2006; I left the recorded tracks in the hands of a music studio executive at Telarc and was not involved in the mixing and mastering. When they sent me the masters while I was on the road, I listened and could hear where people put their own ingredients in the stew. I hadn't been there to watch, so it didn't taste like I wanted it to taste. And Telarc didn't give me an advance or reimburse me for anything. After that I said, "No one will ever be able to do that to me again." Musicians, never leave your product in the hands of anyone. Make sure you're there to examine every step of production.

My dad left a lot of record labels because some were crooked, others were stingy, and some were manipulative. Bernard Besman claimed songwriting credit and publishing rights for a lot of my dad's early songs, including "Boogie Chillen." In fact, it was Besman who filed a lawsuit against ZZ Top for not paying rights to him and my dad for "La Grange," which he lost. Besman and others got thousands of dollars off my dad's work, and they didn't share the royalties. My dad always warned me, "When you get out there, work for yourself. If you don't get your own label, you tell them, 'This is what I want. This is how you got to do it.' If they don't do it your way, hit the highway. Go somewhere else until you get your own." After *Cold as Ice*, I started my own label and called it Steppin' Stone Records because God had used his son, Jesus Christ, as the stepping stone to pull me out of a whole lot of quicksand to sobriety, salvation, and success.

My brother Robert was always good with his hands; he collected refrigerators, fixed them up, and sold them. It was the same thing with cars: he bought them at auction, fixed them up, and sold them. That was his hustle. Over time I started noticing he was mismanaging his money. After my father died, some of my siblings and my mother looked to me for financial support. Robert would call me, saying, "Hey, bro, I need a little help." I would send him money every week or two. Whenever I toured, especially if it was back East or even down South, I would make sure I checked in on him in Detroit. The funny thing was, when I drove into town in our van, he'd always meet me at the gas station—his way of saying he needed some gas. I'd take him out to eat, come by the house, and visit with him; his wife, Lisa; and their daughter LaRorn "Roni" (the older kids had moved out by then). I'd go in the kitchen and sit down; I wouldn't stay long, but I'd drop $200 or $300 and buy them some food, and they'd be very happy. I was happy too. The joy of giving is with me today.

As I kept going to visit, I noticed Robert was getting smaller and smaller, losing weight, which concerned me very much. I loved my little brother; first, we were play partners, then dope and crime partners, and after that, we were both ministers of the gospel. Robert's illness eventually took away his control over his life.

Once, while we were on tour, I found out Robert and Lisa were both in the hospital—in fact, the same hospital where their daughter Roni worked. Lisa was in a coma in one room, and Robert was in another, with one leg amputated. I went to visit him and told him I loved him. I told him I couldn't wait until he was released so he could come out and visit me. Deep down inside, I knew that wasn't going to happen.

He said, "Oh man, I'll be out of here pretty soon. I'm trying to get out of here. These people crazy. I can go home now and take care of myself."

We prayed and I cried. The hospital couldn't legally disclose his diagnosis or prognosis to me, and he didn't tell me; he didn't want me to know. I believe Robert didn't speak about his illness because it would have shown his helplessness. He was a proud man of God.

The following year, Robert was back in the hospital, and he was worse. We were on tour about a thousand miles away and had a few days off; everyone in the band knew Robert, so we drove to Detroit in the tour van. I saw Roni in the hallway, and she showed me to his room. I had asked Roni not to tell Robert I was visiting, and she didn't. It was supposed to be a surprise visit. His eyes lit up when I imitated my dad's stuttering talk and said, "Ba-ba-ba-Minister Robert Hooker, please."

He smiled, laughed, and said, "Praise the Lord. Man, how you know I was here? What you doing here? So glad to see you, bro."

I gave him a big hug and told him I was on tour, had a few days off, and wanted to see my little brother. We laughed and talked about dad, but it wasn't that big laugh you could hear from far away, like before. He was so small and sitting in a wheelchair, with what remained of his legs covered. His hands were so thin and curled up. I did everything I could to keep a straight face. I reached into my pocket, pulled out a hundred-dollar bill, and gave it to him. I wanted to give him a sense of being part of the land of the living and help him anticipate going home soon, but he was just drifting away.

He said, "Oh wow, thanks, man. Don't tell Roni you gave this to me. I don't want her begging."

I couldn't hold back the tears any longer and asked to pray, because I had to get back on the road. While I prayed, I contained my emotions. I told Bob I loved him and hoped to see him again soon. He said, "Man, you gon' see me in Jesus's name. Love you, bro. See you soon. I'll be out of the hospital in about two or three weeks. I'll call you."

I knew he wouldn't. I kissed my baby brother good-bye and walked out of the room with tears flowing down my face, knowing this would be the last time I would see him before heaven.

Several weeks later, I was about to begin another tour, and my mom told me my brother had passed away. He died October 20, 2009, of complications from diabetes; Lisa died of kidney failure around the same time. I was being pulled in all directions: Europe, Australia, Norway, France, Africa, and even Israel. I thanked God for allowing me to see my little brother one more time while he was alive. Because I was all tied up in contracts, I couldn't attend his funeral. If I had, I wouldn't have been able to continue performing and touring, because of the intense emotions it would have stirred up. Of course, I cried and cried. I miss my baby brother—I miss him and Lisa both, especially their very loud laughter.

My musical success continued. Next, I recorded *Live in Istanbul, Turkey* in 2010 with Jazzhaus Records; they had released *Blues with a Vengeance* in Europe. I played dates in Russia, Australia, Casablanca, Tunisia, Tel Aviv, Frankfurt, Munich, and Africa—all over the world.

My booking agent, Intrepid Artists, had me doing festivals with people like Etta James, the Blind Boys of Alabama, and Taj Mahal.

In Russia I remember going to Red Square, and people were protesting. We saw so much police brutality—they were busting heads; blood was spurting everywhere. We got the heck out of there. We played a big festival with about six thousand people in attendance; it was packed. Before we even walked in, two or three of the most beautiful women I have ever seen were standing by the stage door. The guys in the band asked, "Please, boss, can we bring them in?"

I said, "Okay." One of my band members fell so much in love that he bought a plane ticket for one of the women to meet him at our arrival in Turkey. It was so exotically different in Russia; there were people who looked like the KGB protecting us at the stage site. We played two nights in Moscow; people were ecstatic. I'm not beating on my chest, but the most beautiful women in the world were stretching their hands out to me.

When I could, I traveled by train, while the rest of the band traveled in the van, giving me lots of time to write songs for my next album. When I was a little boy, I used to accompany my dad to play a lot of coffee shops. I listened as he told old folklore stories and played his guitar. When I wrote songs, I told modern, urban stories; they are my real-life stories. I used to write letters for the guys in prison trying to get their girlfriends back. I wrote about experiences I'd had with judges, things I'd witnessed in the streets, and things I'd lived. I always had a groove in my head. I presented what I had to Will "Roc," who then brought it to fruition in the studio. The song "Extramarital Affair" on *All Odds Against Me* was about a guy cheating on his wife while on the road, hooking up with girls from Russia. The way I sing "exx-tra marital" with emphasis came from my reaction to him being a habitual cheater. "It's a Shame" came to me when I saw how the downfall of the economy caused people to cheat on each other, bringing big-time corruption into the world. I wrote about real life—not necessarily my life but life in general. I had fun doing it. I can grab stuff from the air and just make up lyrics. It is God's gift to me.

I released *All Odds Against Me* on my Steppin' Stone label in 2008. I toured Europe—France, Germany, Switzerland, and Austria. We did twenty-four shows in Turkey—a trip that was one of the highlights of my career as a musician. We all traveled in a chauffeured bus; there were giant banners with my name on them hanging on the walls of the Hilton Hotels in the different Turkish cities. We played big and medium-sized festivals and theaters. On *Live in Istanbul*, when I began my dad's song, singing, "a-boom, boom, boom," the crowd started singing too—they knew it. My dad never went to Turkey, but they knew his music. We stayed in five-star hotels that had steam baths with fresh hot water from the mountains and amazing food; we were treated like rock stars.

When we drove around, people were glad to see us; they acted like we were from another planet. I wore sunglasses and a hat cocked ace-deuce. We were promoted on TV and radio and in newspaper articles. They thought, "These guys must be superstars." Of course, we weren't, but everybody wanted to take a photo with us.

In Turkey we needed an escort everywhere we went; sometimes we went into different pockets and neighborhoods where there were gangs or people who were anti-American. We walked into one neighborhood, and a gang leader came up and talked to our escort. They wanted to know who we were, where were we from, and what we were doing in Istanbul. The escort said, "This is John Lee Hooker Jr. and his band," and he asked for a pass through the neighborhood for us; they negotiated. The escort told me, "This is a gang leader named Ali. He wants you guys to watch him breakdance and take pictures and film him with your cameras." I said, "Cool. Let's see what the boy can do." He had all his friends and all my guys from America make a circle around him. I told them to turn up the boom box. He hit out doing a breakdance while his boys cheered him on; he was pretty good. When he got up from doing his thing, he had this "How you like me now?" look on his face. I said, "That wasn't nothing. Let me show you how we do it." I challenged him. The escort told him the boss of the band wanted to show him how to really dance, and he said, "Come on!" I broke out to the middle of the circle and did a spin; I mixed it with my calisthenics routine. I did a burpee—when you hit the ground and jump back up—added some mountain climbers, swooped out here, and swooped back there. Ali shook his head as if to say, "Not bad for an old man." We put our arms around each other and posed for the camera, then we were allowed to go on about our business.

We were coming back from Europe one time, and I had my cell phone turned off. After we landed, I turned my phone on, and my mailbox was full. I checked my messages; one of them said, "Congratulations, you've been nominated for another Grammy." Everyone in the band was behind me on the plane. I yelled to the guys: "We've been nominated for *All Odds Against Me!*" The whole plane started clapping. It was something else to be clean and sober when getting off the plane after a long tour, with money in my pocket, then to find out about another Grammy nomination.

The haters said the only reason I'd gotten the first Grammy nomination was because of my name: John Lee Hooker Jr. My manager, Ron Kramer, who produced the Grammy Awards show for about fifteen years and was a former chairman of the board of the Recording Academy, told me, "The academy doesn't take fakes, only originality. They don't cater to names, reputations, or ancestry. They reward only authenticity." So when I got the second nomination, I said, "What do you say now, haters?" That was my vindication: the haters shut up.

My band changed over time; my bass player Big Craig died, and Cynthia introduced me to a sick bass player named Frank "Tebo" Thibeaux. He was instrumental in helping another part of my career. I met a rich Polish man in San Francisco at a Biscuits and Blues show; he said he wanted me to record with his sons in Poland the following year. At the time, I thought, "Okay, just someone's wishful thinking." A year later, he got in touch with me, came to Sacramento, and we made a deal. I started writing songs. Tebo went with me to Poland to record *That's What the Blues Is All About* by John Lee Hooker Jr. and Daddy's Cash; it went straight to gold in Poland.

As for the rest of the band, Will "Roc," who had connected me with Kent Records, helped garner both Grammy nominations. I had Mike Rogers, one of the best and funkiest drummers you'd ever want to play behind you. I named my horn section Hot Sauce: it consisted of Frank Bailey, Doug Roman, and Ric "Mighty Bone" Feliciano, who all also deserve credit for my 2008 Grammy nomination. Jeffrey James was my permanent guitar player and is still with me today on standby should I need him in Europe. Gig Anderson and Elpher "El Dog" Legaspi, both keyboard players, joined us when we were touring after Will "Roc" had left to establish his own band. I believe I had some of the best keyboard players in the world.

After I'd gotten clean and sober, I reconnected with my son Jeremiah, who was in college, getting his bachelor's degree. He would call and ask for money for tuition, fees, and books. I sent him money to put him through college; I felt I owed him. I'd spent the $25,000 I had saved for his education on dope. We were now back as father and son. One time, when my band toured through Des Moines, Iowa, Jeremiah was going to a city college nearby, living in his own apartment and working. I got tickets and rooms for him and Julie—it was a wonderful thing.

Thank God Jeremiah did not follow in my footsteps. After all he'd been through with me, he finished college and began an acting career. He had a role in an episode of HBO's *Power* with Omari Hardwick and the rapper 50 Cent. He and I are close today. I showed him how to do push-ups when he was a one-year-old, and he still goes to the gym, just like I do. One day during the COVID-19 pandemic, we went to the gym together in Roseville and were hitting and challenging each other. I said, "Boy, I'm your daddy. You think you can outdo me?" Yeah, he did outdo me.

While I was on tour and doing a show in Hagerstown, Maryland, I met a Polish woman named Magdalena with a heavy accent; she lived in Washington, DC. I was excited to meet her and invited her to visit me for a show in Ohio. She told her friends and her boss that she'd met me. In fact, she said to her boss, "I know this may sound crazy. I met someone and want to go to his next show. It's in another state." Her boss wasn't supportive. She was nervous and couldn't sleep, not knowing what to do. Her girlfriend encouraged her to go for it. So she flew to Ohio, and I went to pick her up at the airport. While I was looking at the flight arrival and departure screen, someone gently tapped me on the shoulder. I turned around, and this petite Polish woman looked at me with a nervous smile; all she needed was a hug to let her know she was in safe hands. Then this big smile came over her face, and she put her head on my chest and exhaled.

Magda was a beautiful woman, and I'm not just talking about looks— she had a kind heart and a lot of class. We hit it off really well; she was independent and authentic, not a gold digger or a professional groupie. She and I would visit each other in our home states every several months; after about a year and a half, we got married in my backyard by the swimming pool. Jeffrey James and Kim Turner were our best men.

I worked with different promoters in different countries. Magda stayed in Roseville and worked. I called her from the road and told her about what was going on, and she always took care of business at home; she was a smart economist and expert bookkeeper. We played packed stadiums all over the world—eight or nine thousand people in Russia—I was making a lot of money and becoming more well-known throughout the world. Each year, when I came back from touring, I bought a house. In the end, I had bought six of them in the Sacramento area. Magda contributed what she could. Earning a lot of money and trying to become a real estate tycoon wasn't her bag, but she helped anyway.

Michael Rogers, my drummer, and Larry Batiste, the renowned producer, grew up together as musicians. Every now and then, Michael would say, "Larry Batiste told me to tell you he wants to meet you when we come back from tour." I told Mike I'd met Larry a long time ago, when I'd first gotten out of prison. Now he wanted to come to our rehearsal to get reacquainted. He came in and liked what he heard; we started talking about doing a record together. I told him I had my own label, called Steppin' Stone. Later, after we met at his office in Oakland, Larry agreed to arrange, produce, and compose. He is a producer extraordinaire, gifted by God. He is full of honesty, dignity, and integrity and is all-around friendly. If someone wasn't up to his expectations, he told them straight up: "If you can't get this right, then we'll just have to replace you with someone else." I admired that.

We recorded at Pajama Studios in Oakland. Larry called Betty Wright, the "Cleanup Woman," who came in from Florida to record a duet with me called, "I Surrender." Larry directed us: "You pitch and you catch, then you pitch and you catch." At one point Betty went way up and hit a high note beyond my range; I told Larry I couldn't hit that high. He kept encouraging me to try and telling me I could do it. After three tries I said, "I'm sorry, but I can't do it."

Larry said, "One more time, bro. You got this. Let loose." Finally, I hit it. He said, "I told you. You did it."

I had a friend in Paris, Laurent Mercier at Callicore Studio, who made the video for the song "Dear John," which was released as part of the album. I sent him my ideas for the video story, and he sent back the animation; we went back and forth until he landed it. We put out two CDs and a DVD in 2012 called *All Hooked Up*. At the time, video was unheard of for a blues singer. *All Hooked Up* sold like hotcakes and still does at festivals today. Larry and I became very good friends and working partners; he really taught me a lot.

# 20

# MY NEW LIFE IN MINISTRY

My music career was a huge success; I wasn't a superstar, but I was traveling all over the world, and my face appeared on the covers of magazines throughout Europe and America. Not long after being released from San Quentin, I'd gotten two Grammy nominations, a W. C. Handy Award, and the Bobby "Blue" Bland Lifetime Achievement Award from the Jus' Blues Music Foundation. I'd also put out six albums. But the voice of Pastor Dr. Keeton kept ringing in my head: "Elder, you are not an entertainer, you're a preacher. Everyone sees your gift."

It just kept weighing on me every day; the spirit of God would not let me rest until one day, in 2013, when the Lord spoke to me in a loud voice. He told me to come back to the ministry. He said, "I'm not being glorified when you do this type of entertainment. Leave the songs and things of the world, and come back to where you were called: to preach the gospel." I had asked the Lord throughout the years to search my heart and lead me in the right direction. I decided to get out of the music business and announced it to the band. I told them I would do one more year and then I'd be finished with the music that glorified the devil and the world.

I believe it's against my faith to be in clubs serving alcohol, where I'm offered drugs and being winked at by pretty women—trust me, it was very tempting. I love my dad's work; at times, I was covering some of his songs, but I didn't want to encourage people to drink. Christianity is not a legalistic system; there are some dos and don'ts, but God doesn't have handcuffs. We're free to do whatever we want, but we mustn't use our freedom in Christ as a cover-up for evil (Peter 2:16–17). When I sang the blues, it was to please the audience and excite them; I was their Band-Aid, but I was not glorifying God. I didn't want to be seen as two people: a bluesman and a preacher. I didn't care about fame, fortune, or celebrity, so I gave up the world of nightclubs and touring, and I sold my van. I began making music that glorified my God and his son, the Lord Jesus Christ.

One day I told Magda over breakfast that the Lord had told me to get out of the blues music business and go back to the church. At this point Magda and I had been married for nearly seven years. She tried going to church to support me and hear me preach; I give her credit for that. Here she was, this White Polish woman at a Church of God in Christ congregation in South Sacramento, with maybe a few other White people. She seemed very uncomfortable, even though the members of the congregation treated her kindly and welcomed her; it was a kind of culture shock for her, moving from the secular to the spiritual world. Finally, she said, "I can't do this anymore. I have to ask you to divorce me."

I said, "According to the scriptures, I can't divorce you for any reason other than adultery." Because she hadn't committed adultery, I said she had to divorce me, and that's what she did. It was an amicable divorce; she just couldn't accept or make the major adjustment to the new Christian part of my life.

When I asked if she was going to go after all the houses, she demonstrated selflessness and fairness. She could have fought and won half of the five houses that were in both our names. Instead, she said, "No, Johnny, you worked so hard for those houses. They will remain yours." When she asked me, "Do you want your jewelry back?" I said, "No, those were my gifts to you; no one should ever take a gift back, especially if you loved the person and it came from your heart." I just wanted to imitate the character of Jesus Christ throughout the divorce. Because she'd initiated the divorce, the court decreed that she pay me alimony for six months. We settled for the lowest legal amount: $150 per month. When it was time for her to move out, I helped her pack. When she left, she cried; I went in the house and was emotional too. She moved to Virginia, and we remain friends to this day.

The band and I finished up the year on the road; we ended in Europe, with our last event in Tel Aviv. Onstage I gave a brief opening statement about how grateful I was to be in the same country where my savior, the Lord Jesus Christ, was born. As I was talking, I began to be filled with emotion. Just before I started to cry, I said, "Hit it! One, two, three," and the band began to play. I give thanks to Mike Rogers, Gig Anderson, Jeffrey James, and Frank Tebo for knowing when to hit it, how to make my mistakes sound professional, and how to keep playing during my emotional outbursts.

I had a wonderful time in Israel; we all went to the Wailing Wall, where I prayed for God to direct my journey throughout the rest of my life. In fact, my friend Keith Harrell, who was serving a life sentence, asked me to stick a note in the Wailing Wall for him, which I did. He asked God to release him from prison. He told everyone I delivered his note; I don't think anyone believed him.

While I was in Israel, I was contacted by the *Jerusalem Post* for an interview that followed me back to the United States. Because of the article, Pastor Pat Robertson of *The 700 Club* contacted me and asked to shoot a video at my home about my difficult journey and how I'd come to accept Christ Jesus into my life. It was unbelievable! They actually paid me $3,000 to testify about how God had kept me alive and delivered me from all of the dangers of prisons, jails, and homelessness, even after a gunshot wound and a stabbing.

After the divorce and the end of the tour, I hit the ground running. In John 8:32 the apostle says, "You shall know the truth and the truth shall set you free." I was no longer shackled by the devil's drugs; I was back with Jesus Christ and at liberty to do what I love to do. Pastor Keeton said, "I'm so glad to see you back, Elder Hooker. The Lord will see you and establish your gifts wherever you go. He will accept you back as one of his own." I went back to school—I had gotten my GED in Solano State Prison—and enrolled in Epic Bible College in Sacramento in 2015, then received my first educational degree: an associate of arts. I got my bachelor's in counseling and a master's in ministry from Newburgh Theological Seminary and Bible College in Indiana. I also enrolled in a Kaiser hospital program and received a certificate in chaplaincy; the Lord opened a door, and I became a paid hospice and palliative care chaplain, making thirty-eight dollars an hour despite having a police record dating back many decades. The Bible says, "For nothing shall be impossible with God" (Luke 1:37).

One day a letter from Pelican Bay State Prison, a maximum-security facility, came to the church with an unusual request for a preacher to come and assist with the Christmas events for the inmates. Because the pastor knew my background and that I had been a chaplain before, the church secretary gave me the letter. I prayed I would be cleared to go in, and the Lord opened up the gates. I was scheduled to preach and sing two days before Christmas. Pelican Bay is called the End of the World. Most guys don't come home unless it's in a casket. It was a place for gang dropouts, killers, and shot callers—in other words, people that other prison wardens didn't want. I preached, sang gospel songs, and testified about my days in several prisons throughout the United States and Canada. Prisoners can quickly discern if you're a fake ex-con or if you've ever been on the streets. I have witnessed grown men who were chaplains or volunteers come out of institutions crying because they were threatened and told never to come back. The inmates at Pelican Bay accepted me; it was a blessing. Some even knew who I was because I'd known their mothers or fathers. During altar call a young man named Flowers walked up and said, "Chaplain John, you probably don't remember me. I was a little baby when you were our landlord in East Oakland."

I asked, "Who are you?"

He said, "I'm the son of Cassandra and Bobby Flowers."

I couldn't believe it; just before that, he'd told me he had a "double L": double life for two murders.

I was now being trusted to come back into places that had locked me up for almost half of my life. I taught the inmates that there was a God of second and third chances; if he could save me, he could do that for them. The time came for me to go into what my mama used to always call my "second home"—San Quentin Prison—where I was once a chaplain, then a prisoner, and then a chaplain again. Only God can give you this type of favor in the hearts of the untrusting, one-eye-open officers in California Department of Corrections. When I was allowed in, I said, "Lord, look what you have done for me. Look where you brought me from." The Holy Ghost next opened the Sacramento County Jail. I was asked to go to the maximum-security side because it was rough, especially for those who didn't know slick cons: you could get hurt, manipulated, and even killed if you didn't know how to carry yourself. When I was in Avenal Prison in the early 1990s, a snake of a lifer conned a lady librarian, who fell in love with him; she got pregnant in the library and was relieved of her duties. He was transferred to a facility where he'd never get that chance ever again. Another time, my late friend, who I called the cunning Silver Fox, manipulated a lady prison guard in CRC; she fell in love with him and picked him up at the bus station in Riverside. They went directly to a hotel and had sex, then he told her to drive to the dope stroll in Oakland. There he copped some heroin, got hooked, and emptied her bank account. As the Bible says, these are the kinds of men "who worm their way into homes and gain control over gullible women, who are loaded down with sins and are swayed by all kinds of evil desires" (2 Timothy 3:6).

I took the assignment inside the maximum-security section at Sacramento County Jail and ran into someone who'd taken money I'd given him in an attempt to help. When he saw me before Bible study, his face dropped to the floor. He asked to speak to me before we began. With tears in his eyes in front of the whole group, he said, "Chaplain John, I want to ask you to forgive me for cheating you out of the money you tried to help me with. Please forgive me."

I said, "Of course I forgive you," and gave him a hug afterward.

At the end of the service, during altar call, he gave his life to Jesus Christ. How could I not forgive him, especially with all the dirt I have done to folks, even my own family and friends? Look what Jesus has forgiven me for. Jesus said, "For there is nothing hidden that will not be disclosed, and nothing concealed that will not be known or brought out into the open" (Luke 8:17). He got caught even when he thought he had gotten away; he never could have imagined he would run into me at the jail Bible study.

Chaplaincy does not discriminate. God uses people as his mouthpiece, his feet, and his hands to spread his love. Visiting prisons, hospitals, jails, and hospices, I meet people from all walks of life: enemies (including people I broke in the con game), old friends I haven't seen in a long time, and people I thought were dead. Because my reputation had been so bad, some people in prison who ran the streets with me before thought I had conned my way into the penitentiary. When I told them the Lord had changed me, they said, "Yeah, right." The Lord just wants us to plant the seed and keep moving regardless of what people think and whether they accept him or not.

CHAPTER 20

Prison ministry leads you to lots of different people in different places; you just don't know who you'll run into. My friend Jeffery Goode told me about a friend of ours, Robert Foreman, who had been in prison for twenty-five years: they released him from prison because they didn't want to continue paying his medical bills—he was considered hospice material and sent to Alameda County Hospital. Jeffery and I led him to accept the Lord Jesus Christ in his life. We visited killer gang member Tony Rome in an Oakland hospice; Tony had once ordered one of his soldiers to attack me because I'd run off with his dope without paying. He'd also tried to kill one of my friends, Tilden Porter, by beating him in the head with a hammer and leaving him for dead. We prayed for Tony; later he left the hospice and died. I went to Folsom Prison to visit the founder of the 415 prison gang, Mousy Brown, who was convicted of murder; he died in prison of cancer.

I visited my sister Shyvonne while she was in the Sacramento County Jail due to drugs. She was wearing a prisoner's orange jumpsuit. I jokingly told her, "If you run into a girl in there named Big Eugene, a.k.a. Big Genie, tell her you know John Lee Hooker Jr., a.k.a. Magic, and you'll be alright." She held her hand up to her face, changing from sadness to laughter, and said, "You so crazy, Junior." When my sister Karen was in Stockton County Jail on drug-related charges, I went to see her. She was wearing an Alcatraz-type striped jail uniform. When she sat down at the visiting table, she started crying like a little girl. I told her, "You can't let the girls see you crying, or you going to be they sweetheart." Then I said, "Don't worry. If you run into Iron Brassiere Lucy, tell her you know Junior Hooker, and you'll be alright." Her tears vanished, and she busted up laughing. It is our duty to bring the joy of the Lord to the dark places of people's lives, to pray for them, and to introduce Jesus Christ.

Mohammed, "Little Man," was a paraplegic who was shot and paralyzed during a burglary. Our relationship goes back to the 1970s in Santa Rita, when we both learned the con game. Imagine a paraplegic with canes on both arms and who can hardly walk but who is really good at playing the con game. When you play the con game, after you switch the money, you have to hurry. When we played together, I would grab him; pick him up; carry him, running, to the car; and throw him in the backseat. This same brother had been a Muslim who gave his life to the Lord Jesus Christ. After being convicts and dope fiends together, we then both served the Lord. Little Man died, and they didn't have enough money to bury him; I gladly gave the portion of money needed to give him a proper burial.

At San Quentin I saw Charlie Hutchinson, "Too Sweet," who I used to hang out with at the Monroe Hotel. I remembered him as a bully—a mean big old Black guy, always shiny with sweat, who had beady eyes. He wore a crocheted Rastafarian hat ace-deuce. He'd never bullied me, but when he roared, he scared people. After the count cleared, they allowed the volunteers to come in. As I walked in, he looked out the chapel door, noticed me wearing clerical attire, and yelled in a loud voice, "Oh, my God, John Lee Hooker Jr.!" He sounded like he was introducing me onstage in Las Vegas. He said, "If the Lord can save you, I know he can save me too. He can save anybody. Man, I ain't saw you in thirtysomething years."

We talked and Charlie told me they'd given him twenty-seven years; he had five more to go. I'd given him a job back in the days when I had the tree service. He testified to everybody about how he'd witnessed what God had done in my life and now in his; he told everyone I was his partner from the streets. Now I was coming to preach in San Quentin. I went to San Quentin about every sixty days, and he was always there to listen to my testimony. I wrote letters and told him when I was going to preach, and he'd spread the word; everyone from the Bay Area would come in either in disbelief or curiosity. I gave him my phone number; he called collect every two weeks. I looked out for him: this was my buddy who had given his life to Christ. I was so proud of him. It was such a blessing. He didn't have anybody to look out for him, so I sent him money and encouraged him with letters and photos of the ministry.

When he got out, they transferred him to Folsom Prison, and I went to pick him up. He was so nervous about not wanting to violate his parole, he let the guard drive him to the bus station. It didn't offend me; I understood how he felt. He had to wear an ankle bracelet 24/7. They took him to a halfway house.

I gave him some money to get some clothes, and he bought a secondhand suit. I told Jeffery Goode, my good friend from Santa Rita and Avenal, that Charles was out. I had kept up with Jeff, too, picking him up and bringing him to church on Sundays in the 1980s, when I was preaching at Wagoner Memorial. After church, I took him out to eat every Sunday after church. When Jeff's quality of life was at a low point, I was his friend and never looked down on him. Now Jeff and I went to pick up Charlie from the halfway house to take him to Jack in the Box; he was so happy to be free and was looking around everywhere he went. The women were catching his attention, but he forced himself to take his eyes away. Charles asked, "How do I get a Coca-Cola out of this machine?"

I said, "You got to yell into the machine. The computer will take your order, and then it will fall out."

He yelled, "One Coca-Cola?" and we burst out laughing; he had been away that long and wasn't familiar with the digital age.

Jeffery told me, "You wrong, John," and we got him the Coke.

Then Charlie asked, "How can I get a hamburger, a cheeseburger, or one of them big burgers right there?"

I said, "You got to walk out to that window around at the drive-through, and just go stand next to the car."

Jeffery said, laughing, "No, don't do that!"

Oh boy, we had fun! That's how long he'd been locked up: he didn't even know how to order at Jack in the Box at the order screen. Even now, he doesn't know how to send a text message on a phone.

Charles was so excited. He joined a church in Oakland called Alpha and Omega. He testified to the pastor about us going back to the 1970s and me being a prison chaplain. He got involved in his church, and the pastor invited me to preach. After I finished preaching, testifying, and singing, they blessed me. One ex-convict, Mario Gaines, came out; he and I ran the street, shot dope together, then did time together in Santa Rita. Now he's Bishop Mario Gaines.

One day I was ministering at Pelican Bay, and in the middle of a Bible study, an inmate asked if he could say something. I said, "Sure."

He said, "Chaplain Hooker, you may not remember me. I'm from Oakland. One day you tried to play the con game called the pigeon drop on me."

As he was talking, I jokingly reached into my pocket and asked, "How much do I owe you, sir?" Everyone burst out laughing. He said, "You don't owe me anything. I didn't fall for it." More laughter erupted. I knew I'd gotten him for some cash, but he just didn't want to admit it—that would've made him look like a mark inside of a prison. The guys would have said, "Man, you a sucker."

People who'd seen me on the streets know the authenticity of my story; they know the realness. For others, I've sometimes had to pull up my sleeves and show my tracks. They look at me, stunned: "Oh, my God."

Back when I was touring, I went to Alaska every year, like clockwork. This went on for about ten years. One day the promoter, Frank Dahl, called me from Alaska and said, "It's that time of the year again. Let's book these events." I told him the Lord Jesus Christ was back in my life, and I wouldn't be doing this anymore. Two years later, that same man stopped drinking and accepted the Lord Jesus Christ in his life. Frank read about me on Facebook, about my going into San Quentin and Pelican Bay as a chaplain. He was known all over Anchorage; he called me and said he could get me into Hiland Mountain Correctional Center, Lemon Creek Prison (in Juneau), Spring Creek, Goose Creek, Anchorage Correctional Facility, and Wasilla State Prison. He flew me over for ministry and took care of all my sustenance and hotel accommodations for three years in a row. I thank God for Frank Dahl, my partner and brother.

While I was in Alaska, one lady walked up to me and had this look on her face. She said, "I want your autograph." She was holding a flier she'd removed from the wall of the prison. She said, "I was there when you performed in Anchorage with Bo Didley maybe ten years ago. Now I'm meeting you again in prison, and I want your autograph again." Many emotions rose in both of us.

Another time my manager, Ron Kramer, told me someone from a theater in Texas wanted to book me in Houston, and Ron told the promoter I was a prison chaplain. The guy said, "Well, I know the pastor of the church. Let me see what I can do." He spoke with the pastor, who said, "I'll be out of town, but my pulpit is open, and my staff will be there to accept him." He also had a connection in Jefferson County Texas Correctional Facility. I preached and played my gospel event with a local pickup band and backup singers, and the next day, I went to the jail. I met two or three guys who were in there for murder; I told them about how God had turned my life around. When they heard about a second chance and I told them God could do the same for them, they began to smile and thanked me with big hugs for coming to talk with them. The sheriff had a camera and took photos. We were all just one big family. I told them, "I love y'all, man."

When I was visiting the Phoenix Penitentiary, all the inmates came in, and one guy rushed up to me. He said, "Chaplain John Lee, I've been waiting for you for a long time. You and I were in Jamestown together in 1976 or '77," and he gave me a hug. He said, "Now I know Jesus is real."

It was special for both of us. You can go into the prison system and be a liar or a fake, but someone will expose you as a pretender. The God I serve would never have allowed me to serve in prisons if I were a hypocrite or had wrong in my heart. I came to tell the truth.

At the California Medical Facility in Vacaville, I was preaching and five guys from my time in the streets and from Santa Rita came into the church. After the service was over, they all walked up and asked, "Remember me?" and introduced themselves. I remembered all of them. After those guys left, another guy came up, Ronnie—six feet, nine inches, with a crutch. He only had one leg because he had gotten into a fight with a Crip inside a cell in San Quentin. The guard had tried to break it up, telling them to stop, and then blew Ronnie's left leg off with a shotgun; he ended up in Vacaville. He asked me, "You don't remember me?" but not in a nice way. I looked up at the guy and kind of recognized him. Before I could say anything, he said, "I'm Ronnie, Tee Tee's cousin." I said, "Help me out. I can't remember." He said, "You robbed me." I said, "If I robbed you, I hope you can forgive me."

He said, "I'm going to chalk that up as a loss and to the game."

That got him in trouble. Someone went back and told the Oakland set this guy had confronted Chaplain John Lee Hooker Jr. I was told that when he went back, he was checked real hard and warned not to ever do that again. There were BGF and old-school 415 still locked up in there; they respected my transition from the streets to the pulpit. They'd heard I had changed my whole life, and they didn't like him confronting me like that, especially in the church. They made him respect me.

During this time my mother had moved from Berkeley and was living in a house in Sacramento I'd bought for her. She would still snap her fingers while giving orders, but her health was declining. She didn't move like she used to; she still cooked for the family and on big occasions, but she needed assistance. I visited her every two or three days, making sure she had groceries; we went shopping together. She joined a church around the corner from her in Sacramento, but she had trouble going, so I took her. It was a blessing to see her as much as I could. Every time we got back to her house, she grabbed the wall to pull herself up the first step, but she had to take another step to get into the house. Her ankles were swollen, and it was difficult for her to move.

One day she called me and said, "Junior, I can't make it up these steps anymore. It's becoming really difficult. I'm getting ready to go to Diane's and live there. I can't do it no more by myself."

I said, "I got your back, Ma. Don't worry about nothing. I'll make sure you're comfortable. Matter of fact, I'm going to give you my new car so you can drive while you're down there."

My mom moved in with Diane, who was living in North Edwards, California, out in the Mojave Desert. I took my car down there and took a train back. After a month I asked, "How's the car running?"

Diane said, "Junior, Mama can't drive the car anymore. Mom ain't doing good. I'm putting her in this one room so she can be really comfortable. We need some new carpet in that room."

They knew how I was about my mama. I said, "Alright, go pick it out at Home Depot. Don't pick expensive."

Of course, she got the most expensive carpet they had in the store; it was over $1,800. But that was for my mother; I wanted her to be comfortable. I flew down to Bakersfield or Los Angeles and took a bus out to North Edwards, and they picked me up. The car was just sitting in the front yard, full of dust. I saw my mom's room, and it was beautiful. I told her how much I loved her, gave her some money, and spent a day with her. I was so busy, I couldn't stay long. I drove the car back home to Roseville.

One day Kathy, a promoter from the Cannery Casino in Las Vegas, called to book me; she had booked me there before and was under the impression that I was still singing the blues. I told her that I was no longer singing those types of songs, only the gospel. She said, "John, you can't sing about Jesus in Las Vegas."

I said, "Kathy, that's what I do now. But I tell you what, it's got a funky sound." She took a deep breath and said, "Okay, John," and she booked me for June 2016. My friend Calvin, who'd been in Moriah House drug rehab with me in Redwood City, was living in Las Vegas in a church recovery place. He told his pastor about me—he loved to brag about his buddy. The pastor and I got in touch, and I was invited to preach on Sunday after doing the gospel event on Saturday.

By now my mom's illness had progressed, and she was lying in and couldn't get up. She had no appetite and wouldn't eat; she was looking off into space, just like I remember Big Mama used to do. I knew her demise was imminent, and I was about to take off for Las Vegas, so I went to North Edwards and brought Karen, her daughter Danielle, and Jeffery Goode with me. When we got there, I went into the room where Mom was lying on her bed, put my face on her face, and told her, "I love you so much, Mama."

She said, "I love you, too, Junior."

I told her, "Mom, you know you're going to heaven when this is over."

She said, "I know that, boy," in a tone that said, "Duh, who you think you talking to? Of course I'm going to heaven when I die."

You have to have certainty; you have to believe your name is in the book of life. I know I'm going to heaven when I die as well. I gave her a kiss and shed a couple of tears. Karen was with me and did the same.

After that we jumped in the truck and drove to Las Vegas. I did the event at the Cannery Casino, and at around two or three in the morning on Sunday, June 16, we got the call from Diane: my mom had died of ovarian cancer. You could hear Karen and me both crying from down the hall. She called me and said, "Junior, Mama gone. Try to get some rest," but nobody could sleep. I got up, took a shower, and met my sister before breakfast. She said, "She want us to be strong, bro. Come on. We got work to do."

I preached at the church on Sunday, and I think I handled it pretty well, considering what I had just been through. I was the preacher in the family. I also asked one of my friends, Dr. D. C. Carter, to sing at my mother's funeral at her church in Sacramento later on. A lot of people from my church, Progressive Church of God in Christ, showed up to support me. I looked around at them; it is so beautiful when the saints are there for you in times of sadness.

# 21

# SINGING ABOUT
# THE LORD

In 2017 my manager, Ron Kramer, called me a couple of weeks before I was leaving for a tour in Europe and said the promoters for the Rolling Stones wanted to know if I could do a thirty-minute set to open for them at the Red Bull Ring in Spielberg, Austria. I thought, "Lord, look what you are doing. This is my opportunity to glorify, magnify, and lift up the name of Jesus." I said to myself, "Because I'm going to sing the gospel, this may be the last time they ever call me. I'm going to sing to the honor and glory of the Lord." Jeffrey James Horan, my guitar player, and I went, while the rest of the band—DiCarlo, on drums; Ramni Krishna, on bass; and Carly Quiroz, on keyboard—waited in Berlin for the tour to start. This was the largest concert I had ever been a part of: there were 140,000 people.

The Stones had their own restaurant and their own fleet of Mercedes Benz sound trucks; they flew in on a private jet from Munich. This was the mecca of concerts, with a stage with a runway that ran fifteen to twenty yards out. I was told during sound check that I could only go out to where a white line was drawn at the five-yard line: the rest of the runway was for Mick Jagger. I knew my place, and I was thankful and humbled to be a part of this giant festival. The word of God says, "When someone invites you to a wedding feast, do not take the place of honor, for a person more distinguished than you may have been invited" (Luke 14:8). This was the most famous rock 'n' roll band in the history of the world!

The stage was set, so the announcer gave us the signal, and Jeffrey James introduced me; when I went out, I felt no butterflies or nervousness in front of the hundred thousand or so people who were there, waiting for the Stones. My dad had prepared me for this moment. I just thought, "The bigger the crowd, the more ears to hear the gospel of Jesus Christ." Our set consisted of only three songs. I started with "Maudie," a song my dad wrote about my mama—a real Hooker pleaser—then I sang "Amazing Grace" and "Praying," a song I'd made up with Jeffrey James back in the dressing room. Singing my dad's song "Maudie" was really meaningful for me. He wrote it in 1959 and always said it expressed his true feelings about my mother, even after she left him when I was a child. It has a real laid-back groove, and in the lyrics, he declares his love for her. But the lyrics also say that she's been gone and ask why she's hurt him. The song is so personal to me because of the feelings it expresses. I had to catch myself and fight back tears when I was singing "Amazing Grace," for it was because of God's grace and mercy I wasn't on dope or killed by another gunshot. If I thought too much about where I was, how I'd gotten there, and how the lyrics told my story, I wouldn't have been able to sing. When I got to "Praying," a basic twelve-bar blues with a shuffle beat and improvised lyrics, the crowd began to clap, cheer, and, at my beckoning, say, "Hallelujah!" and "Glory to God!" while lifting their hands and arms in the air. What a miraculous experience to see thousands waving their hands to heaven; I felt the hand of God was using me to fulfill the scriptural command of Jesus Christ: "Go into all the world and preach the gospel to all creation" (Mark 16:15).

After I'd left the stage, a great rock band called Kaleo, from Iceland, went on. We were escorted to our dressing rooms near the restaurant for staff and musicians. Someone with the Stone's production company came by the restaurant and said, "Mr. Hooker, Keith Richards would like you to come to his dressing room to meet you and say hello." Keith Richards was an old friend of my dad's. They'd performed together on television, and Keith had visited my dad's home in Redwood City. Of course, I took Jeffrey James with me so maybe he could get Keith to sign his guitar.

When we walked into Keith's dressing room, he was seated on a long couch, and his manager, his wife, and a few assistants were there. In his thick accent, Keith said, "By Joe, it's Junior Hooker. You look just like your daddy, ol' boy. John would be proud of you. Come and sit down over here, next to me. So I hear you are a prison chaplain, aye?" He told me funny stories about him and my dad, even imitating his stuttering, and talked about the fun they'd had in the hot tub and partying. We stayed for about fifteen minutes, as Keith had to get ready to go on.

Before we left I asked Keith if I could say a prayer for him and his band. He said, "You know what John Jr., I think I need prayer." His entire crew gathered with Jeff and me in a circle, and we all held hands. I prayed God would preserve and protect them from all hurt and danger and he would change all our lives. Most of us said, "Amen." As we were leaving, Keith said, "If we ever need you again, Junior, we know where we can find you . . . and that would be in prison." We both let out a loud laugh when he said it; he knew about my ministry and that I had spent time in prison. We embraced and took some photos together; Jeffrey got his guitar signed, and we left.

The promoter gave us notice that we were going to have a photo shoot with Mick Jagger, Ronnie Wood, Charlie Watts, and my new friend Keith Richards. The five of us gathered in a room; Mick and his boys were all smiles and very kind. The photographer had me stand between Mick and Keith and shot several photos from different angles. It was another day at the office for them, but for me, it was a grand slam, a day the Lord had made possible, and I was so glad. At that moment, I wished my dad was alive to see me brushing elbows with his old acquaintances, the Rolling Stones. He would have said, "Reverend Junior, look at you, boy. Now don't get the big head. You gone go farda then dis. Just don't go back down that road again, you know what I mean." Those words from him are embedded in my mind forever.

He would have told Keith, "Look out for my boy. He's a preacher now, Keith. Don't introduce him to none of yo gurls eder. And don't offa him no weed." The next day, we flew to Berlin to begin our gospel tour with Sid Tevis and Elder P. Sylvester, who were supporting me on the road, with the permission of our pastor, B. L. Toliver.

In 2020 I recorded my gospel album, *Testify*, at Infinite Studios, owned by Michael Denten. Eddie Mininfield played saxophone, and Charlie Musselwhite, who'd played with my dad and me back in the days when I'd opened for my dad, had reconnected with me at the San Francisco Blues Festival. The producer for that album was the legendary Larry Batiste. I had so many great people on the album: Alvon Johnson, Wilton Rabb, and Jeffrey James Horan were all on guitar; then there was Dick Bright on violin, Troy Lampkins on bass, Sylvester Burks on keyboard, Michael Rogers on drums, Juan Escovedo on percussion, and Jeanie Tracy, Omega Rae Brooks, Bryan S. Dyer, and Claytoven Richards, all on backup vocals. I had a horn section with Bill Ortiz, Doug Rowan, Brad Catania, and Ric "Mighty Bone" Feliciano. There are songs of worship and praise on the album. I especially like "His Holy Name." In that song I give glory to my Lord Jesus Christ and all he has done for me. I sing stories about being shot, stabbed, and homeless, as well as being on drugs and in prison, but I always add in scripture. I testify about what I went through: how he brought me out of the pits of hell, from the kingdom of darkness to the kingdom of Jesus Christ. It's a victorious album about redemption and second and third chances.

We did two videos for the album; on "My God Is Holy," the cast is phenomenal. Larry Batiste invited most of his friends, including the legendary Pete Escovedo; his son Juan, who was on percussion; and his son Peter Michael, the videographer. On the studio version of the song, I had Elder Don Carter; Elder Paul Sylvester; Larry Batiste; Missionary Icealicia Tolbert; her mom, Sherri Tolbert; Missionary Debrah Madden; and Herman Phillips, all on vocals. On the short video directed by Erin Galey, which was filmed inside the Progressive Church of God in Christ, we had Frank Tebo Thibeaux on bass, Gig Anderson on keys, Cliff Murrey on guitar, and Mike Rogers on drums. It was joyous to be able to incorporate all those voices and even choir singers from the church. Jeffrey James describes it better than anyone: "There's some funk, there's some blues sound, there's some zydeco, and there's some musical narration, but the good news of the gospel stood out of it all."

My dad was a storyteller. Shirley Caesar, the gospel singer, was a great storyteller. And I'm a storyteller too. Even back when I played the con game, I was telling stories. One time in Oakland, on the first of the month, after people got paid, I went out with a mish, a knot wrapped in a paper bag, rubber bands around my wrist, and a nail in my pocket. I saw a guy who had just cashed his check; he'd climbed in his car, shut the door, and started his engine. I stood in front of the car and waved for him not to move. Then I went up to the car window and held up the nail for the guy to see. He rolled down the window and told me how grateful he was, believing I'd saved him from a flat tire. I started my story about how I was lost and looking for this hotel but was afraid to take all this money over there to retrieve my key. I told him I needed help. I said, "I can't make you rich, but . . . ." He had $900 in his wallet from cashing his paycheck. I played the usual con game and took off with the money. After I'd rounded a corner, knowing he would look inside the paper bag and freak out, I saw a car parked in a driveway in front of a garage and crawled under to hide. About five minutes later, I could hear the engine roaring and racing as he kept driving around the block at high speed, looking for me; I stayed under that car for forty-five minutes and got away with the money.

Like in the con game, I tell stories in my music, both back in the day, when I was singing the blues, and now, when I sing gospel. Even when I testify, I tell stories about myself—and about others. Now that I sing gospel, the stories are true. Before altar call, you have two choices: repent and accept Jesus Christ, or say no and live eternity in damnation. I often tell the story about my buddy Keith Harrell, who was offered ten years in a plea deal. I told him to take the ten years.

He said, "You talking like them White folks. Man, I didn't rob them people."

I told him he may not have robbed them, but he did something. I advised him, "Accept the ten so you can get back home!" But he didn't.

He went to trial and got forty-five years; he was sixty-one years old at the time. Today as I write, he's seventy-two. It was a life sentence for him. I say, "You don't have to be like Keith. You need to accept the plea bargain right now: life in heaven or a life in hell forever. The Lord Jesus Christ will give you eternal life; if you repent and follow him, all your sins will be cast behind. He will wipe your sin record clean."

I tell people they have to save themselves, like on an airplane, when the flight attendant tells you to put on your oxygen mask first and then help those around you after. I tell a story about two guys on a safari who see a hungry lion. One guy straightens his shirt, his pants, his hat, and ties his shoes. The other guy says to him, "What are you doing? You can't outrun the lion."

The other one answers, "No, but I can outrun you."

Salvation is an individual choice; save yourself first. My family, friends, jailers, prison guards, lieutenants in San Quentin Prison, and even the devil told me, "You'll always be a dope-fiend loser. There is no escape." I came to believe it. I went to jail month after month, year after year, for most of my life. It was an ongoing cycle. We tend to believe there is no hope for us, so we continue to do what we do because there is no change. So when someone like me comes back from the dead, as it were, and says, "Look at me; I made it," it is encouraging to those who have been through what I've experienced. I'm not trying to be sanctimonious; I just know God can do anything because he alone has set me free from all the vices and habits and given me a right mind.

# 22

# SHARING LOVE AND LIFE IN GERMANY

The word of God says, "A good name is more desirable than great riches; to be esteemed is better than silver or gold" (Proverbs 22:1). God alone is the reason that my name is no longer infamous or untrustworthy; promoters no longer had to stipulate in their contracts, "No drinking before or during the show." My mother and sisters no longer had to carry their purses to the bathroom. My name became respected all over the world in music, in the streets, and among family, friends, and even my enemies. God told me to return to the people I'd hurt to compensate them. It was not to pay them back for the wrong I had done them but to be a blessing where I was once a curse. There is a story in the Bible about a rich man named Zacchaeus, who was a chief tax collector. He wanted to see Jesus, but he couldn't, because of the large crowd. By faith he climbed a tree so that he could see the Lord. Jesus saw his efforts and changed him; he promised to pay back all the people he had cheated (Luke 19:1-10).

After my dad died, some of my family members began to rely on me financially, and I was glad about it. I'd stolen Robert's gun, Karen's Atari, Lavetta's color TV, Shyvonne's typewriter, Zakiya's pistol, and my mama's rent money. The Lord blessed me to be able to put a roof over the heads of three of my sisters as well as my mother (in a home she shared with Shyvonne). After I had squandered Jeremiah's college fund on drugs, I was able to purchase a condominium for him and attend his college graduation, when he received his bachelor's degree. I had robbed and stolen from my best friends. Bowlegged John and I played a mark one time, and I ran off with all of the money—but today we are best friends. The Lord helped me take former San Quentin associates Kim Turner and Sonny Hill off the streets. I bailed Kim out of jail and brought him; his wife, Sonita; and Calvin Williams to Sacramento, where I rented them a house to get them off the streets. Twenty years later, I moved Calvin into my home for a short period of time; later I was made his official caregiver by the Department of Veterans Affairs. This was the same man who took care of me when I arrived, sick and malnourished, at the Moriah House drug program.

From the five homes I purchased with money made while touring in Europe, I unfortunately took a loss, as I only rented to people no other landlords would rent to: the underprivileged and those with bad credit scores. When they didn't have furniture to move into their homes, I purchased secondhand furniture. I brought them a bag of groceries from free-food day at our church. Some people, even those in my family, said I was crazy. They said, "Why are you doing this? People don't do those type of things." It was the Lord's doing, and it was marvelous. I give him all the glory and praise; without him, I could not have done anything.

Eventually, Sonny overdosed on drugs, fell into a coma, and moved to a nursing home because of brain damage; Kim had a stroke. As a friend and chaplain, I was there for their spiritual support. The holy scriptures say, "If anyone has material possessions and sees a brother or sister in need but has no pity on them, how can the love of God be in that person?" (1 John 3:17). As a chaplain for the Lord Jesus Christ, I find all my assignments are driven by his love and compassion. Sometimes I'd leave a hospital or nursing home in tears; other times, in joy. That was the case when I visited Mom Helen, the mother of my bass player, Frank Tebo. She smiled when we arrived and announced to the nurses, "This is my other son, John Lee Hooker Jr." I also had the blessed opportunity to visit Mom Doshia, the mother of my keyboard player, Will "Roc." She was sitting in her chair next to the receptionist. When I began to talk with her about Jesus and to pray, her face transitioned from a stoic look to one of joy, and she said, "Preach!" That is what the word of God calls pure religion: "Religion that God our Father accepts as pure and faultless is this: to look after orphans and widows in their distress and to keep oneself from being polluted by the world" (James 1:27).

One day one of my friends I'd done time with called me from prison, asking, "Have you found a new wife yet, Brother John?" And he asked me how long it had been. I told him eight years.

He said, "Wow, Brother John, you act like you're still in prison with us, man."

Trust me, I was burning inside like a man who's on a desert island and hasn't had a drink of water for a long time, but I was waiting for God to send me the right woman. One Sunday my good friend Dr. Don Carter said in his closing remarks over the microphone, "Chaplain John Lee Hooker Jr. is a single man and is looking for a wife. Please pray for him." I almost melted in my seat and looked for ways to disappear. Because of his announcement, one sister waited for me on the inside of the church and another, on the outside. I smiled and went directly to my car. The best place for a man to find a wife and for a woman to find a husband is inside the church, but even there, a person still needs to be careful; not all those inside the church are saved. I remembered that the scriptures have been my best weapon in spiritual warfare against the tricks of the devil.

After all those years of fending off enticements and fighting my own desires and temptations, one day I was reading the responses from a testimonial comment I'd made on Facebook and noticed a familiar name that wasn't American but German: Birgit, pronounced "Beer-git." I responded and asked, "Is this my Birgit?" It was a friendly question, not flirtatious; she answered, "Yes."

I first met Birgit at one of my shows in Hanover, Germany, in 2004. She was with her husband and her young daughter. It was the first time her family had ever seen me perform. I had a website back then, and they'd written a letter asking for an autographed photo. When they got to the show, they identified themselves and had a photo of me at the Grammys that they'd downloaded for me to sign; they brought it over to the table. I give glory to God I'm a friendly person and can get along with folks. I remember all the people trying to get to see my dad, and the bodyguards would say, "You're not coming in."

My dad would say, "Let him in; come on in, son," or "Let the lady come into the dressing room."

The bodyguard would say, "Are you sure, John?"

And he would say, "Let him in."

I have the same attitude: just welcome people, be kind—you're not a superstar, you're a human being. My dad used to always say to me, "Don't ever get the big head, now. People can't see you because of your big head." He had some corny country sayings, but they were so true.

CHAPTER 22

So they all came to the table, and I heard Birgit's husband say a negative-sounding something to her in German, but I didn't understand. I could tell she didn't appreciate it—his words seemed to really upset her. When he went to the bar to get some drinks, I grabbed her hand and said, "It's okay. You're going to be alright. I don't know if you understand me, but take care of yourself. Know I'm your friend, and God bless you."

Two years later, in 2006, Birgit and her daughter came out to another event; now she and her husband were separated, and she was very happy. I was newly married to Magda, but I was still Birgit's friend. We exchanged emails periodically after that, just friendly notes and pleasantries. Birgit was and is a very shy person. She didn't speak very good English, and of course, I didn't speak German, but we understood one another.

About twelve years passed, and because of my faith, I'd left the promotional company that booked tours in Europe. I wasn't singing blues anymore. By now I was doing prison ministry all over the United States; I testified on Facebook about how the Lord was doing marvelous things in my life. That's when I saw Birgit's name and sent a quick message. After she'd told me it was the same Birgit, she wrote, "I read all these stories about you and how you have changed. You have the Lord in your life. It's so wonderful."

We started talking over the phone. By then I had been alone for eight years. She'd been through two divorces and was living in a small apartment by herself. On September 11, 2018, Birgit shared with me that she'd been feeling like she didn't want to live anymore; she asked me to pray for her, adding, "How can I find Jesus too? How can I change?"

All it took for me as a preacher was to hear those words. When we are in our extremity—at the lowest part of our lives, at the bottom of the barrel—that is when God presents his opportunity. The Lord told the Israelites, "You will seek me and find me when you seek me with all your heart" (Jeremiah 29:13). I believe the Lord read her heart and guided her, in his providence, to me because he knows me; he knows our needs.

I told her the Lord was going to change her if she believed. I asked her what religion she was. Birgit said she was Catholic. I was honest with her and told her what I believe. I said, "Mary is not perfect; she is not to be worshipped." Some Catholics believe Mary, angels, and priests are mediators for their sins, but I believe "there is one God and one mediator between God and mankind, the man Christ Jesus" (1 Timothy 2:5). We prayed, and I asked the Lord to touch her heart. I told her, "He is the mediator between man and God, not a priest, not Mary, and not the saints. The Lord is going to change you. Do you believe Jesus Christ came to this earth through the birth of a virgin, Mary, and died on the cross at the age of thirty-three, that he rose from the grave and went back to heaven and is coming back again?"

She said, "I sure do."

I asked, "Do you know what repentance means?"

She said, "No."

I replied, "Repentance means to change directions from this lifestyle to a lifestyle consistent with the Lord Jesus Christ. No, we're not perfect. We're going to fail. But the scriptures say, 'If we confess our sins, he is faithful and just and will forgive us our sins and purify us from all unrighteousness'" (John 1:9).

She said, "Well, I've been smoking since I was twelve years old."

I said, "I was smoking when I was eleven, and the Lord took the cigarettes from me—and the drugs and the nightlife and the cursing."

She asked, "How will I do that?"

I said, "You're just going to ask the Lord Jesus Christ. A preacher's not going to marry a woman who's smoking and drinking and hitting the clubs every night." I was just thinking in terms of any preacher living in Germany—not me in particular—but somebody she might meet.

She asked, "You would marry me if I quit smoking?"

I said, "I didn't mean I would marry you. What I meant was that if you want to marry a Christian or a preacher, you can't be smoking with a bottle in your hand and going out to the nightclub every night." I then asked, "Are you ready to give your life to the Lord Jesus Christ and live for him the rest of your life?"

Birgit then started crying.

I asked, "Do you believe?"

She said, "Yes, I do."

I asked, "Are you ready to repent? Are you ready to turn from all the smoking, the drinking, the discotheques, and all the evil, for Jesus?"

She said, "Yes, but it's going to be hard."

I said, "Yes, but nothing's too hard for God." I testified to her about my life and was shocked when she said, "I already know. I read about you all the time on Facebook."

I realized she had been following me for years.

Birgit accepted the Lord Jesus Christ into her life. I told her, "The spirit of God will help you change. Be sure to get down on your knees every day and pray to God, and he will help you. You don't have to go cold turkey when you try and quit all those habits. Just ask God to take it away; things you used to do will become distasteful to you. I'm going to be praying for you as well."

I stayed calm on the outside, but on the inside, I was emotional; I had no idea what the Holy Ghost was doing, except that he was using me to lead someone to the Lord.

Just to give a sense of how serious she was, Birgit contacted a Protestant pastor named Adreas Pauly and told him she would like to join the Protestant Church. The pastor came to her apartment and talked to her. I told her what to say to him: "Let him know you believe that the Lord Jesus Christ is the creator of the world and is God himself." After she'd spoken with him, she became a member of the Evangelisch (Evangelical) Protestant Church. She then contacted a Catholic priest to give notice that she was leaving the Catholic Church. When the priest came to her apartment, she spoke with him about the Virgin Mary and how we have all sinned; she explained that no one is perfect except Jesus Christ. He was very nice and gave her his blessing.

Weeks and months passed, and in 2019, Birgit had a vacation coming up; she called to tell me she was coming to San Francisco and asked if I would show her around. I kind of knew she was infatuated with me, as I was with her. Plus, I was single, but I let her know that nothing could happen romantically. She said she understood. She asked if I could pick her up; I told her she could stay in my house in my guest room. I didn't have any type of motive; I served Jesus Christ.

Birgit was shy, a little withdrawn, and quiet; she didn't socialize much. But I thank God that she wasn't loud or sassy talking and she didn't curse. I picked her up in San Francisco; she was so happy, just smiling and beaming from ear to ear. In her broken English, she said, "I have quit the smoking no more." She said she didn't even have the urge to smoke or drink or go to discotheques anymore. She said it was truly a miracle and that even her friends said she had changed.

I showed her around the city, we went to dinner, and then I drove her to my home in Roseville. I saw a very happy person who had never been to America before. About two weeks later, she was sitting by the pool, drinking coffee; when she stood up, I pushed her in. She giggled like a little child. I wanted to show her a good time.

She said, "I want to go to Florida, to Orlando, to see the dolphins." She wanted me to go with her and offered to pay; she was very generous. I hadn't planned on going to Florida, as I'd been to all those places before. But because she was so excited to go, we went to Orlando so she could watch the dolphins and have a good time. I could see she was like a big kid; she smiled and laughed. She took pictures with the dolphins and everything else she hadn't seen before.

After we came back from Florida, I was scheduled to go to Pelican Bay, near the Oregon border, as part of prison ministry. She gladly came along; I got her a room with points I'd earned from staying at Best Western Hotels. While I was at the prison, she went down to the Pacific Ocean. She had never seen blue water; the North Sea just looks like dark mud. She was so happy, walking by the ocean.

One day, while she was sitting at the patio table next to the pool, I asked her, "What is it you want from me, Birgit?"

She said, "I just want to be happy."

I went to the back room, shut the door, and got down on my knees. I prayed, "Lord, who is it you have for me to be my wife? Is it another? Should I wait?"

The Lord said, "That's her right out there, sitting by the pool."

I went out, sat by Birgit, and asked, "What is going to make you happy?"

She said, "You know what would make me happy."

I asked her, "Would you be my wife?"

She said, "You have get on knee one," or something like that—it was broken English. So I got down on my knee and asked, "Would you be my wife?"

She said, "Yes," with a smile and tears on her pretty face.

The next day, we went straight down to Sacramento City Hall and got married. The word of God says, "He who finds a wife finds what is good and receives favor from the Lord" (Proverbs 18:22).

I took her to church, and she was happy. Birgit stood up when she heard the gospel music and was clapping with everybody, even though her timing was off. She enjoyed herself; she had never been on the inside of a Holy Ghost–filled gospel church, where people dance in the Holy Spirit and shout "Hallelujah." I could see the tears coming down from her eyes. It was an amazing moment.

That same day, Elder Beaumonte said from the pulpit, "We'd like to thank God for Elder Hooker and welcome Sister Hooker here to our church." Oh, did he preach! After services, most of the sisters lined up to greet Birgit and give her a hug. She was impressed by the kindness that was shown to her from all those Black folks; she had never in her life experienced such a moment.

Birgit returned to Germany in November 2019; I was supposed to perform on a tour of Germany in March 2020, but the pandemic struck. The tour was canceled, which meant I wouldn't see my new wife until it was over. Birgit and I were brokenhearted. I flew to Germany in November 2021, and we renewed our vows at her church so her family and friends could be there to see me put the ring back on her hand. I preached at a scheduled event at the church; it seemed like everyone had come there to see this American brother with gold crowns on his front two teeth who'd married a woman from Cloppenburg.

When the Lord told me she was the one, I'd thought she would come to live in Roseville. But then I asked the Lord, "What should I do?"

The Lord said, "You're getting a little older. Her mother and father are still alive, and yours aren't. You go to Germany to be with her." I didn't ask, "Are you sure, Lord?" Instead, I made an announcement to my family, my church family, and my friends: I was moving to Europe. I sold my house, gave away some clothes, and sold some furniture, then gave away the rest. Within ninety days, I moved to Germany. Paul said, in the spirit of God, "Do nothing out of selfish ambition or vain conceit. Rather, in humility value others above yourselves" (Philippians 2:3). I packed my suitcases, confident that it was the voice of the Lord guiding me. God called Abraham and told him to leave his country and all his kinfolk and go, but God didn't say to where. I knew where I was going, but still, for a Black man to go to another country . . . .

I returned to the United States in December 2021 to sell my house and move to Germany.

Before I left for Germany, Charles Hutchinson came to hear me preach in Oakland at the Christian Fellowship Center, hosted by its pastor, Dr. Gerald Agee. He was struggling to adjust but hanging in there.

I told him I'd met this wonderful woman I had known for eighteen years and I was moving to Germany. He asked me, "What are you going to do with your truck? How much you going to sell it for?"

The Lord told me to give Charles that truck. I said, "It's yours, brother."

When I came back from Germany to preach in the States, Charles was at the airport to pick me up in the same truck. There were chicken legs on the floor. He said, "Today, I'm your escort."

I said, "No problem. Drop me off at the hotel." A light had been broken, but that special engine in the truck still sounded the same. That truck's still rolling, and he's still wearing with dignity the same $150 hat I'd given him. He's a special man.

Birgit had a little bitty apartment in Cloppenburg that had a tiny green bathtub and downstairs neighbors with a barking dog and crying baby. What a change from a swimming pool, marble and granite surfaces, Tiffany-colored glass in the living room, and a TV on the wall in every room! As the traditional hymn goes, "Oh, what a change in my life!" It took two or three weeks for all my things to get to Germany; I had pallets of belongings. While I was getting ready to move, Birgit rented a house with four bedrooms. We had never before rented a house together. She filled out the application, and the people gladly rented the house to her.

The Lord began opening doors like I never could have dreamed. I preached and sang in St. Josef Catholic Church, backed by Cloppenburg's own Jazz Stompers. I also preached at Evangelisch Church, under Pastors Pauly and Maria Eva Burke in Cloppenburg; at Hamburg International Baptist Church, under Pastor Edgar Luueken; and at the church in Idar Oberstein, thanks to Christian Herzig. In Oschersleben in East Germany, I preached in an old converted pig stall because Pastor Holtz and his wife, Angelika, didn't think the little church in the village would be able to hold the anticipated crowd. They had never had an event like this before. It was a small village, but the place was packed. Six or seven months later, promoters from NASCAR Europe somehow got in touch with the pastor of that church. They were looking for someone who could pray, sing the American national anthem, and knew something about cars. The pastor said, "I know just the man. His name is Reverend John Lee Hooker Jr. He preached and prayed for us and sang. Plus, he's from the Motor City, car capital of the world."

The marketing director for NASCAR, Alexandra Werner, said, "We'll take him."

This was the third major sports event I had been asked to host in my career. First, I'd been on Fox for March Madness college basketball around 2004; next, I'd been the voice on CBS Sports for Worldwide Tennis, promoting Serena Williams and Roger Federer in 2008.

On September 23 and 24, 2023, my assignment was to pray for the NASCAR drivers and fans; say, "Gentlemen, start your engines!"; sing the national anthem; and sing while the drivers were taking a break. I was also to present the trophy to the winner. They treated me like I was from the White House, like I was in the royal family—people from the embassy in Berlin were there, and cameras were everywhere. I took photos with the Oschersleben football team. It meant a lot to me to be called to a big event as a preacher.

In 2022, after the pandemic, the guys in my former band in Berlin called me; they were down and out. With no demand for live music for a long time, they had bills to pay. DiCarlo, my drummer, called and said, "John, we know you love the Lord, but can you please do this one last tour for us?" I knew I was strong enough not to be tempted on the road by drugs or pretty women; I also knew it was the kind, selfless, and considerate thing to do. People were going through hard times because of COVID-19, so I agreed to do a twenty-seven-day tour in Germany. We went north, south, east, and west: Hanover, Berlin, Hamburg, Frankfurt, and Munich—all over, to some really nice venues. Everywhere we played was packed. I testified about my life, how the Lord Jesus had brought me over the hills and through the woods. In my songs I would ad lib about how I used to use drugs. In one song, "Listen to the Spirit," I would tell them, "The Lord will tell you drinking, smoking cigarettes, and using drugs are no good. He will tell you to treat your wife or girlfriend with respect, like the queen that she is. He will tell you to honor your mother and father"—all to a groovy beat. During the break the hotel manager at the beautiful Hotel Bayerischer Hof, in Munich, told me, "I have never in my whole career as manager of this hotel heard somebody come in and talk about their life and the Lord Jesus Christ. Thank you so much. They needed that. I am a Christian as well." I was pumped; this was my confirmation from the Lord.

After my wife, Birgit, had gone to great efforts to assist me in getting a German ID and then, miraculously, my driver's license, we hatched the plan we had long prayed about: God blessed us to buy a house in Cloppenburg. The Bible says, "Every good and perfect gift is from above, coming down from the Father of the heavenly lights, who does not change like shifting shadows" (James 1:17). Looking back at my life, I wonder who would've ever thought John Lee Hooker Jr.—the thug, crook, thief, con player, drug addict, convict, and bum—would end up owning property in Germany with his German wife? Not only property, but a beautiful, completely remodeled home with three bedrooms, an office, three bathrooms, and eleven-foot hedges out front, surrounding the entire home! It is like the homes I saw in Beverly Hills, when I escaped from Synanon. One bedroom has a balcony where you can look out over the little community, which is named after a Catholic priest. It's quiet and has privacy, a model area to live, just like my dad taught me. God has put me in this home with a beautiful person whom I will love for the rest of my days. People in the community know there's an American preacher by the name of Reverend John Lee Hooker Jr. living here. Birgit and I are two peas in a pod: I'm a Black American preacher and musician, and she's a simple girl from Germany. We seem like opposites—and we are—but we are held together by the spiritual DNA of the Lord Jesus Christ.

Living in Germany, I'd say one of the things I miss most from my life in America is ministering inside the places that had held me most of my life: prisons. The scriptures say, "Take delight in the Lord, and He will give you the desires of your heart" (Psalm 37:4). My wife and I prayed for almost three years for the Lord to give me the opportunity to enter German prisons for ministry. One evening, after arriving back from the United States, we stopped to have dinner at a restaurant; as we were waiting for our dinners, I opened my email and saw the subject "Good News." The message was from Dr. Meins Coestsier, from Fulda Prison in Germany, telling me I had been cleared to go inside. The visit was scheduled for December 12, 2023. Glory to God, what a time we had! Reverend Andreas Leipold met me, then took me inside for sound check and to introduce me to the other staff members: the priest, the guards, the choir, and the primary person in charge, the warden. While I did my sound check, Reverend Leipold, who was dressed in his clergy clothes, began to dance. I could see the prisoners up above, in their cells, clapping their hands in anticipation of being let out after the count cleared.

After I was introduced, I told the inmates, in German, I was happy to be there. Switching to English, I testified about how I, too, had been in and out of jails and prisons for almost forty years. I told them how the Lord Jesus Christ had set me free and how he is coming back again. Then I said in German, "Jesus loves you, and so do I." There was a round of applause. A couple of the guys grabbed one another and started dancing and joking. Before I said my farewells to the prisoners in German, I sang one last song that I prayed would resonate in the hearts of those who listened: "Let That Devil Go." The ending lyrics say, "If you want to go to Heaven, you got to let that devil go."

While I was visiting, I noticed the prisoners were allowed to smoke; I mentioned to a guard that smoking isn't allowed in US prisons, and he said, "We believe in humanity." The prison food was also better; I was led to the front of the line and had some good sausages and dessert. The prisoners had on uniforms, not the yellow or orange jumpsuits found in the States but uniforms with nice jackets and shoes. I think inmates are treated much better in Germany. There was no tension; everybody got along.

The next day, my wife and I received an email from Reverend Andreas Leipold telling us how impressed he was by my visit and informing me that he'd written to the large prison in Hünfeld, recommending me for their Theater Behind Bars program. He'd also contacted people working on the music festival Hessentag in Fritzlar that brings about 700,000–800,000 people to the town. Hallelujah! We received the approval. I preached, sang, and told my story at the Stadtkirche Fritzlar for four days during the festival, from May 30 to June 1, 2024.

Being John Lee Hooker Jr. is a blessing and a curse.

I had the opportunity to open for my dad and play with him. I had the chance to go on tour with him, and even when I was high, stealing from opening acts, and trying to feed my addiction, I still had the chance to tour the United States and Canada, as well as perform live in Soledad Prison. When I was finally clean and sober, he recommended to me his guitar player, John Garcia, who played with me when I first started out. In those early days, I'm sure the name Hooker helped open some doors. People are curious: "I wonder if he's anything like his dad?" With my name, I've had people take a look at me. But just having a famous name doesn't mean the talent was passed on. People tried me, and I had to prove myself.

On the curse side, there was always pressure to live up to the honor of the name. On two occasions while I was in prison, my dad's music came on. The first was in Wayne County Jail, and "Boom, Boom" played on the radio. The second time was when I was in maximum security at Big Greystone in Santa Rita Jail and my dad was on TV. The guys said, "Man, that's your dad. What are you doing in here?" I just wanted to shrink, but I smiled. All the attention was on me, and I don't like attention. I have been too low to the ground to be comfortable with anybody looking at me as a celebrity. But when I preach, I am doing something I was inspired by the Lord to do. I enjoy trying to get people out of their current conditions.

As I reflect back over my life, I know that it's a miracle I'm alive today. I overdosed, was stabbed, was shot twice, and even had a shooter ready to shoot me (instead, I'd covered my head with my hand, which he then hit and broke). All that I can say about my destructive past is that had it not been for Jesus, I'd be dead and gone. My life was in quicksand, and the only one able to pull me out was my savior, the Lord Jesus Christ.

King David said, "I waited patiently for the Lord; He turned to me and heard my cry. He lifted me out of the slimy pit, out of the mud and mire; He set my feet on a rock and gave me a firm place to stand. He put a new song in my mouth, a hymn of praise to our God. Many will see and fear the Lord and put their trust in Him" (Psalms 40:1–3). Thanks be to God for blessing me and getting me out of the shadow of the blues.

# NOTES

## INTRODUCTION

1. Most translations of biblical verse cite the New International Version.

## CHAPTER 2

1. For information about songwriting credits, royalties, and the lawsuit, see Charles Shaar Murray, *Boogie Man: The Adventures of John Lee Hooker in the American Twentieth Century* (New York: Penguin, 2000), 119, 154–56, 345. For Music Corporation of America's (MCA) payments to artists, including Hooker, for the back catalog it acquired, see Richard Harrington, "MCA to Pay Royalties to RB Greats," *Washington Post*, December 6, 1989, https://www. washingtonpost.com/archive/lifestyle/1989/12/07/mca-to-pay-royalties-to-rb-greats/63714098-29be-481e-915f-cb43f6bdf07c/.

## CHAPTER 3

1. Al Wilson, "The Snake," Soul City, vinyl, 7 inch, single, 45 RPM, released August 1968.
2. For information about Reggie Harding's life and death, see, "Reggie Harding, 1942–1972," *Detroit Free Press*, November 12, 1972, 13; as well as Branden Hunter, "How the Cruel & Unforgiving Streets of Detroit Swallowed Up Reggie Harding," *MichiganPreps*, September 19, 2017, https://michiganpreps.rivals .com/news/how-the-cruel-unforgiving-streets-of-detroit-swallowed-up-reggie -harding.

# CHAPTER 4

1. Ionia Correctional Facility is a maximum-security state prison in Michigan.
2. Jackson State Prison was the first prison in Michigan, the largest walled prison in the world.
3. Billy Joe Royal released "Cherry Hill Park" on the Columbia label in 1969.

# CHAPTER 5

1. For an overview of Synanon, see Hillel Aron, "The Story of This Drug Rehab-Turned-Violent Cult Is Wild, Wild Country-Caliber Bizarre," *Los Angeles Magazine*, April 23, 2018, https://www.lamag.com/citythinkblog/synanon-cult/.
2. For more on Dederich's legal woes, see Lawrence Van Gelder, "Charles Dederich, 83, Synanon Founder, Dies," *New York Times*, March 4, 1997, https://www.nytimes.com/1997/03/04/us/charles-dederich-83-synanon-founder-dies.html.

# CHAPTER 6

1. For information about Cassidy Lake prison camp, see Lucas Smolcic Larson, "From 'Happy Living' to 'Fence It or Close It.' The History of a Prison Camp near Chelsea," *MLive*, January 22, 2023, https://www.mlive.com/news/ann-arbor/2023/01/from-happy-living-to-fence-it-or-close-it-the-history-of-prison-camp-near-chelsea.html.

# CHAPTER 9

1. Santa Rita Jail is on the site of the former Camp Schumacher, a World War II US Naval base that may have housed Japanese POWs. Before it was a navy base, it was the site of a prison farm; for more information, see https://www.norcalbailbonds.com/history-santa-rita-jail-dublin-ca.

# CHAPTER 17

1. For a history of the Boom Boom Room, see Joel Selvin, "Boom Boom Room Opens with a Bang," *SF Gate*, October 4, 1997, https://www.sfgate.com/entertainment/article/boom-boom-room-opens-with-a-bang-2803324.php.

## CHAPTER 19

1. Lyrics from Shirley Caesar with Reverend Milton Brunson and the Thompson Community Singers of Chicago, "Hold My Mule," *Live . . . in Chicago*, Rejoice Records, 1988.

2. Lyrics from Shirley Caesar, "Satan, You're a Liar," *Rejoice*, Myrrh MSB-6646, 1980.

# ACKNOWLEDGMENTS

## FROM JOHN LEE HOOKER JR.

To my very special lady, my God-sent wife Birgit Hooker—you and me baby, 'til death do us part and we see each other in glory. Mein wunderbar Schatz, ich liebe dich. To my two sons, Gerry and Jeremiah, you are my two jewels. To my little sister Karen, you are my road dog. To my funny-style nephew Reesie, from your funny-style Unk, love you boy. To Lavetta and my late sister Diane, thank you for being my anchor. To Zakiya and my late brother, Robert Hooker, I miss you, Preacher. To my spoiled sister, Big Bonnie; to my late gospel dad and pastor, Dr. L. W. Keeton; and to my teacher and pastor, Dr. B. L. Toliver of the Progressive Church of God in Christ (COGIC), thanks for your wisdom. Thanks to Sid Tevis, Elder P. L. Sylvester, and my European support, Elpher "El Dog" Legaspi, you bad, dude. To Jeffery Goode, you were always there with me, both chained and free. To Minister James "Cry James" York, stay close to the cross. To Kim Turner and Sonny Hill, you're my oldest partners. To Christian Herzig, you are special. To Karl Heinz, Jürgen, and your wife Ulrike, thanks for your kindness. To Prelate Bishop Mario Gaines, thanks for elevating me to International Chaplain of COGIC. To servant Pastor Joseph Jones and First Lady Danielle Jones, thank you for your welcome sign for me at Alpha and Omega. Thanks to Pastor Freddie Jackson and his wife Jodie and to the entire Chatmon family at Wagoner Memorial COGIC. To Steve and Dr. Kirkland, thanks for everything—I love you. I thank God for Frank "The

Bank" Dahl for opening the doors to ministry in eight prisons—'til we meet again my friend. To my manager of twenty-six years, Ron Kramer, you have been a booster shot to my career; thanks for your guidance. Special thanks to the bass specialist, Darryl "Funky Z" Fields; Frankie Bailey on trumpet; Ric "Mighty Bone" Feliciano on trombone; Doug Rowan; and Angelo Santi on guitar. And thanks to all of the multitude of musicians from all over the world who have assisted me in my career. Thanks to my cousin Archie Hooker for being there for my dad, and to my big sister Francis McBee, thank you for your kindness.

Special thanks to Alexandra and Markus Werner of NASCAR for allowing me to participate in NASCAR Europe again in 2024. To Pastor Andreas and Angelika, I love you both. Thanks to Chicago Dave, Jacob, and Johannes. To Carol Wavely, my great neighbor, you helped me in many ways. To Viva Fitness; Demitri Dingis; Viktoria "Vicky" Katharina, my sister in the Lord partner for life; Anika, and Marion Siemens, thank you for your kindness. To LaRorn Hooker, you are special to my heart. To Kaiser Hospital chaplains, Dr. David Roth, Chaplain Wade, and Chaplain Ruel Guerrero, as well as Professor Charles Williams and Dr. Ronald Harden of Epic Bible College, thanks for your training and teaching. To Callicore Production in Paris, France, and especially to Laurent Mercier, thank you for the great animated cartoons. To Dr. Gerald Agee and First Lady Alesia, thank you for your kindness and for opening the doors to your pulpit. To Jacky "Bo" Grote, Lil' Dejan, and Nico, thank you for your acceptance of me. To Mom Helga and Dad Heinz, thanks for your daughter's hand in marriage. To Michael Tan, I want to thank God for you, sir. This project had been sitting on a shelf for over a decade without any oxygen until you came along and took it off the shelf, giving it breath. I am forever grateful to you. To my coauthor, Professor Julia Simon, for tolerating me during the most difficult times in writing this book; you showed kindness, patience, and professionalism even in adverse times. To Herb Harris, my childhood friend, thanks for your helpful information for this book. Special thanks to my sister in the Lord, Leslie Olivares, for all of your encouragement.

To my new clergy and Christian brothers, sister, and friends: Pastors Andreas and Imke Leipold, Rev. Dr. Fabian Vogt, Rev. Deiter Dersch, and Parviz "P. V." Amir Ali, Pastor Thurnell Clayton—thank you for your guidance and encouragement. To Larry Batise, thanks for your belief in me and for your wisdom and guidance. To Darryl Newell and Dodie Hultz, my two friends for life—wow—how you helped me! To

Warden Clark DuCart, thank you, and to my friend Mr. Robert "Mr. Bob" Losacco, the relations manager at the Pelican Bay Maximum Security Prison, thank you for opening up the gates, doors, and cells of the prison to me. To the late Missionary Yancy and my cousin Pastor Albert Featherstone, thank you for inspiring me to become the chaplain I am today.

To all of the men and women of Barracuda Music GmbH—Michael Genrich, Christian Leyrer, Florian Mittermann, and Ewald Tater of Nova Music—I'm so grateful to all of you. To Dirk Stolzenberg of Fabulous Concerts, many thanks, my friend.

To my Lord and Savior Jesus Christ, thank you for your long-suffering grace and your unprecedented love. Lord, thank you for saving me, sanctifying me, and filling me with the Holy Ghost. None of this would be possible without you. Thank you for this story that we will use to promote your great name all over the world, so that men, women, boys, and girls who are suffering from addiction, living in the streets, and doing time in prisons will know that there is deliverance in your name! I give you all of the praise and the glory, again, thank you, Jesus!

## From Julia Simon

Thanks to Reverend John Lee Hooker Jr. for sharing his life story with me and entrusting me with bringing it to the page. Thank you to Adam Gussow, for making the introductions; to Ron Kramer and Michael Tan, for your help and support; and to my family and friends, for your advice and encouragement.

# ABOUT THE AUTHORS

**Reverend John Lee Hooker Jr.**, born in Detroit, Michigan, is the son of blues legend John Lee Hooker. As a teenager, John Lee Hooker Jr. toured with his dad, opening his shows as the featured attraction. He also had the opportunity to record with his father live at Soledad Prison in 1972. But as a result of drug addiction, he spent several decades in and out of jails and prisons, including Soledad. Overcoming his addiction, he then had a successful career as a blues artist, receiving two Grammy nominations and the Bobby "Blue" Bland Lifetime Achievement Award. Now an ordained minister, Reverend John Lee Hooker Jr. performs contemporary gospel music in- and outside of prisons.

**Julia Simon** is Distinguished Professor at the University of California, Davis, and the author of *Time in the Blues* (2017); *The Inconvenient Lonnie Johnson: Blues, Race, Identity* (2022); and *Debt and Redemption in the Blues: The Call for Justice* (2023).